REPRODUCTIVE
WRONGS

ALSO BY SARAH RUDEN

Perpetua: The Woman, the Martyr

I Am the Arrow: The Life and Art of Sylvia Plath in Six Poems

Vergil: The Poet's Life

The Face of Water: A Translator on Beauty and Meaning in the Bible

Paul Among the People: The Apostle Reinterpreted and Reimagined in His Own Time

Other Places (poetry)

TRANSLATIONS

The Gospels

Confessions: Augustine

The Greek Plays: Sixteen Plays by Aeschylus, Sophocles, and Euripides
(Agamemnon, Libation Bearers, Eumenides)

Hippias Minor or The Art of Cunning

The Golden Ass: Apuleius

The Aeneid: Vergil

Homeric Hymns

Aristophanes: Lysistrata

Petronius: Satyricon

REPRODUCTIVE WRONGS

A Short History of Bad Ideas About Women

Sarah Ruden

A Division of W. W. Norton & Company
Independent Publishers Since 1923

Copyright © 2026 by Sarah Ruden

All rights reserved
Printed in the United States of America
First Edition

For information about permission to reproduce selections from this book, write to Permissions, Liveright Publishing Corporation, a division of W. W. Norton & Company, Inc., 500 Fifth Avenue, New York, NY 10110

For information about special discounts for bulk purchases, please contact W. W. Norton Special Sales at specialsales@wwnorton.com or 800-233-4830

Manufacturing by Lake Book Manufacturing
Book design by Chrissy Kurpeski
Production manager: Anna Oler

Library of Congress Cataloging-in-Publication Data is available.

ISBN 978-1-324-07590-5

Liveright Publishing Corporation, 500 Fifth Avenue, New York, NY 10110
www.wwnorton.com

W. W. Norton & Company Ltd., 15 Carlisle Street, London W1D 3BS

Authorized EU representative:
EAS, Mustamäe tee 50, 10621 Tallinn, Estonia

1 2 3 4 5 6 7 8 9 0

*To three champions of this unusual book:
my dedicated and talented agent Gail Hochman;
Dan Gerstle, who boldly acquired the book for Norton;
and Maria Goldverg, who devotedly edited it*

CONTENTS

PREFACE ix

1 DAWN OF THE DICKS
  *The Roman Imperial Poet Ovid Inaugurates
  Antiabortion Propaganda* 3

2 PREGNANT AND FOOT-WASHING
  AND IN THE KITCHEN
  Early Christian Reproductive Backlash 33

3 IT'S THE BABY, STUPID
  Augustine's Neurosis, Our Theocracy 63

4 HAMMERED
  A Monk Off His Head About Women's Bodies 85

5 HELL'S BELLS
  Dickens Shills for Victorian Misery 107

6 THIS LOOKS ODDLY FAMILIAR
  Eugenics and the Holy Image 137

7 YOU *CAN* MAKE THIS STUFF UP
  Antiabortion Messaging in Wonderland 167

ACKNOWLEDGMENTS 191
NOTES 192
SELECTED BIBLIOGRAPHY 203
INDEX..................................... 208

PREFACE

THIS BOOK WAS CONCEIVED FROM THE SUSPICION that I—a translator, literary critic, and cultural historian—had something to offer in the fight for reproductive freedom in the United States: a perspective on how long and how exuberantly communications campaigns against this freedom have been going on. I now hope that it proves empowering for readers to find out what our ancestors faced in their media—especially when it looks a lot like what we are facing in ours.

Since at least the late first-century BCE—I am looking only at Western cultures because that is my expertise, and because the Western tradition has, of course, most powerfully shaped the present American political crisis—authorities have shown a particular reliance on propaganda for opposing decisions people try to make in their own interest about their own bodies and families. Only with abominable slowness did the hard truths of life-shaping experiences come face to face with officially sanctioned fabrications and manipulations.

When I began this book, it felt rather ridiculous that I, a person trained on Homer and Vergil to be a highfalutin Classical philologist, should be weighing in about one of the crudest sequences of political writings ever to manifest; then it began to feel less ridiculous. I recalled how, during my forty years of work in languages and literature, I had constantly struggled to glimpse, through the artifices of words, what some of the canonical figures of Western civilization *really* mean when they speak. I found standard translations of important works dull, obscure, and suspiciously compliant with the dominant ideologies of the eras in which the translators lived. In my own translations I strive to represent the original authors' thoughts and artistic achievements more clearly, which requires pushing back constantly against my mental and emotional habits as a modern American.

The deep skepticism I have developed in this way may help explain a direction I took after my return twenty years ago from a long sojourn in Africa. I began listening seriously to devout Evangelicals and Catholics—people not at all popular with the academic family in which I grew up, the Classicists who taught me, and the Quakers who are my religious community. In 2010, I published a book, *Paul Among the People*, that appealed to conservative Christians, and in time I was speaking at some of their institutions and conferences and writing for some of their magazines. Many of the people I met during this period had views on traditional values that resonated with me. I felt that such values involved a healthy caution about human wisdom, goodness, and power in the face of rapid technological innovation and social change. Not only had studying the ancient world through its literature offered me a foundation from which to critically examine the direction that modern life was taking, I had also spent ten years in the new South Africa, where I was surrounded by old cultures that continued to bleed from their arteries as reactionary impositions were replaced with radical ones. Back in America, I was ready to listen to people who claimed to represent the wisdom of tradition.

But the logic I heard from religious conservatives concerning reproductive choice came to alarm me: Since crisis pregnancies are a powerful argument for legal abortion, the religious right did not permit crisis pregnancies to exist. Every fetus everywhere on earth was supposed to be deeply loved and fervently wanted, and if human evidence of this did not materialize, then proof by faith must step in: God loved and wanted the fetuses, and so God's providence would prevail—and if it didn't look like that was happening, our limited human view was at fault. Again and again, I heard people insist that women must rearrange their lives around this formula.

Whenever I challenged this viewpoint, I ran into a strict and seemingly unique ban on discussing it, so that I began to suspect that I was dealing not with an ordinary moral or theological principle or cultural preference, but rather with an obsessive political goal. About everything else—including the Pauline doctrine of salvation itself—I found that Evangelical and Catholic leaders were at least willing to talk, and often willing to tolerate dissent. For instance, in a university run by an extremely conservative Protestant denomination, some faculty sported signs on their office doors signaling a willingness to listen to gay and lesbian students in confidence and without judgment. But whenever I argued against an absolute abortion ban, nothing came in response but evasions. When I explored what antiabortion activists and true believers were saying to each other, at exclusive gatherings and in inward-directed media, I found a conviction that only a ban on abortion could force a corrupt and decadent society to return to strict morality based on the godly nuclear family; moreover, those in the antiabortion movement who expect the end times to arrive soon hold that the war against abortion is a critical clash between good and evil that prepares for the second coming of Christ. The antichoice movement has become a fanatical religion in its own right, complete with a loopy futurist mythology.

Many people were baffled after the US Supreme Court overturned the constitutional right to abortion, and the abortion bans that resulted in certain states were so harsh that some women were even denied emergency care for miscarriages and emergency contraception after rape. Surely, the mainstream public thought, the authors of these new laws and the conservative judges tasked with enforcing them would relent when they realized what was happening. Surely they would rush to amend and enjoin, assure doctors and nurses that they wouldn't go to jail for following the medical code of ethics and saving women's lives. Surely women would not have to dread the kind of reproductive totalitarianism that Margaret Atwood depicts in *The Handmaid's Tale*. Many thought the US could and should go the way the rest of the world was going, toward a compromise in family-planning policy. To political moderates everywhere, there seems to be a natural balance between women's rights and the rights of fetuses that are healthy and developed enough to survive outside the womb. Why should pregnancy be the single realm of wildly skewed legal and moral absolutes, the realm in which, for example, the right of an expiring fetus to exist for another hour trumps the right of a woman to her normal lifespan?

But it is now clear that conservative courts, legislatures, and media have dug in their heels, and even turned their backs. I think that is because, well, this is the United States. Here, the peculiarly Western evolution of radicalism still rampages free, wreaking havoc. In the West—and reaching out from it—authoritarianism has depended, basically and characteristically, not on control of key material resources (like the Pharaohs' control of irrigation water), or sheer violence (like that of the Golden Horde that established the Mongol dynasty), or on the religious awe rulers exact (as in the Inca domain or Czarist Russia), but on extensive overhaul of thought, on persuading people to behave in strange new ways that are supposed to serve the needs of their very special polity and its just claims to power. The enduring vigor of Western authoritarianism is rooted in language, language that infiltrates and manipulates popular participation. To Americans, overambitious power, when it arrives, may not feel like the king's tax collector, the overseer with his whip, the chieftain's raiding party. This power may not feel alien, hateful, to be thwarted when possible but otherwise submitted to. This power may feel like part of us. It feeds on our own fervent convictions, on ideology.

Today, the clinging, burning effects of ideology, a sort of political and social napalm, are reaching a crisis. And ideology surrounding reproduction is very special in its power-hunger. About fertility, even more than about sex, those in power have been able to make things up, and their audience has almost never been able to answer back. To do that seems to require not only destroying their own privacy but also exposing their children to unspeakable truths, such as that they were not wanted.

The silence women have borne along with children is very deep, and understandably so. Oblivious to this, or just determined to take cynical advantage, men and their female agents bully women and their partners and entire supportive communities rhetorically, with the language of lofty, authoritative certainty about this most intimate and consequential part of life. It was, for example, preachily explained to Christian women during the early second century that they must pursue spiritual salvation through confined, submissive, obedient childbearing; only men, apparently, could be saved by faith. Not long afterward, it was decreed that the female body was the gateway to hell; only by denying herself sex and motherhood could a woman rise to heroism in God's eyes.

We probably shouldn't feel any relief that such bluntly brutal doctrines are out of fashion. In the distant past, authoritarians' stated ambitions were often in inverse proportion to what they could actually do. As I show in my first chapter, antiabortion propaganda began under the first Roman emperor, Augustus, probably in connection to his pro-natal and pro-family laws. But there is no evidence that anyone heeded the propaganda, and the laws were widely dodged. There were no resources, and there was no popular will, for invading privacy on the scale that was called for. The emperor only presaged the state's forceful interference in women's intimate lives.

My second and third chapters are based on the New Testament Pastoral Epistles and the writings of Augustine, respectively. The language used would suggest near-totalitarian measures on the ground to force childbearing in the first case and prevent it in the second. But instead of pointing to systematic abuses of couples' reproductive autonomy by the Christian hierarchy in late antiquity and the early Middle Ages, I can mainly cite theology and doctrine, with which a great many Christians probably fell willingly into line.

The power of words to foment organized reproductive violence manifested only in the age of early printed books and the restless, rising commercial classes, who demanded some rationale for what their clergy and local rulers were doing. During the early-modern witch-hunting craze, which I explore in the fourth chapter through the blockbuster tract *The Hammer of Witches*, young fertile women and midwives were the witch-hunters' main victims, and their alleged main crimes were breeding Satan's army with demonic lovers and using contraception and abortion to prevent the birth of God's army. The campaign against witches lasted for hundreds of years in widespread outcroppings and a couple of concentrated centers (German-speaking Central Europe and Scotland); the ratio of deaths to prosecutions was horrifying (the Spanish Inquisition was far less murderous); and the terror tactics were so impressive that the profession of midwifery, and women's traditional right to manage their reproductive lives with a degree of privacy, took centuries to start recovering.

By the nineteenth century, meddling in fertility, though much less direct and violent, was common, and even had an air of bustling, philanthropic entitlement. And again, and more pervasively as literacy grew, writing was an indispensable vehicle of the meddling. Authorities appear bent on raising the birthrate to get more low-wage labor by means such as a medical pressure campaign—heralded by pompous books—against the nonreproductive sex act of masturbation. Young people made to feel shame and terror when they took care of their urges alone and in private were drawn to early marriage as an alternative and inevitably produced more children than did couples who married late. The most popular author so far in history, Charles Dickens, supported the authorities with his heavy-handed prescriptions for early marriage and large families even for people on the edge of destitution. His novella "The Chimes" offered shockingly callous messaging of this kind. Propagandistic language was working its full magic, making people believe that what was bad for them was good for them. At this stage, such language was the proverbial velvet glove covering the iron fist, as the nineteenth century saw the first draconian laws against abortion, which cracked down on female contraception too, since at the time there was no verifiable distinction between preventing a pregnancy and ending a very early one.

By the early twentieth century, eugenics was dominant; its proponents in their trendy writings could sound humanitarian, or even mystical and romantic, like the British Marie Stopes. I explore one of Stopes's most influential, most bewitching books, *Radiant Motherhood*, in detail. But some of the public policy results that eugenicists achieved were brutal, including the forced sterilization of girls and women deemed (on little or no evidence) "imbeciles" or "morally insane." Much worse, eugenicists contributed to the greatest collection of crimes in human history. They wrote the script for the Nazis, who instituted breeding programs for the "Master Race" alongside the industrial-scale killing and enslavement of other peoples.

In the late twentieth and early twenty-first centuries, in the purportedly advanced and democratic United States, many soft-pedaling, pop-culture types of antichoice propaganda have appeared. I explore the biography of the "abortion survivor" with the pseudonym Gianna Jessen. By a sort of paradox, this propaganda-lite serves new, extreme ambitions for control and punishment. Without minute reproductive surveillance, a sci-fi dystopian level of medical interference, and a Kafkaesque penal system, it would be impossible to—in those sweet, conscientious-sounding words—"protect life from the moment of conception."

Never before has there been a greater disconnect between what we may be facing and how it is being sold to us. It is time to take seriously the moment in which we find ourselves and the cartoonist Walt Kelly's dictum that we have met the enemy, and he is us. Our greatest conflicts are no longer fought over our heads with bombs and terrorist hijackings. We fight them ourselves with our communications, and we can prevail, securing a humane and decent life for ourselves, only if we take a more careful account of what exactly we are hearing and what it actually means.

REPRODUCTIVE
WRONGS

CHAPTER 1

DAWN OF THE DICKS

*The Roman Imperial Poet Ovid
Inaugurates Antiabortion Propaganda*

IN AMERICA, WE'RE USED TO HEARING CONSERVATIVE pundits claim, often pointing for support to our cultural foundations, that it is "natural" and "moral," as well as advantageous, for a couple to have as many children as they can. This is how it was supposed to have been in the good old days.

The evidence of the long period of Near-Eastern and Western antiquity, when people worked out how to survive in large, complex, settled societies in southern Europe, northern Africa, and southwestern Asia, evokes a loud "Duh!" to the contrary. In a period critical for the development of our heritage, from the eighth century BCE to around 500 CE (best known through the records of the Greek and Roman civilizations), much of the region in question was already deforested, dried out, and less than ideal for a human population that continued to grow. Adding to the widespread immiseration were the wars hungry polities waged on each other. The Greeks and Romans believed (and paleoanthropologists back them up) that the good, prosperous, peaceful time was the Golden Age before agriculture and trade, when the heartless plow had not yet wounded the earth or the greedy keel violated the sea. The Jews held, similarly, that this time was before Adam, expelled from Eden, sweated to wrench food from the resistant earth.

The Jews had only one very fertile tract of land, the Jezreel Valley, and their small territory as a whole was an invasion highway and buffer zone for mighty empires—Egyptian, Assyrian, Babylonian, Persian, Macedonian, Roman. In the historical period, the Jews did not practice child sacrifice or infant exposure, and Hebrew scripture attests to a passion for fertility in both men and women. Jesus, "the only son of God," reportedly had six siblings. Long before his time, families too large to hang on to subsistence-size plots of land from generation to generation had been a factor in poverty, political instability, and vulnerability to catastrophic foreign crackdowns. In 70 CE, the Romans prevailed in their siege of Jerusalem, destroyed the Second Temple, and slaughtered vast numbers of Jews; vast numbers of others were sold into slavery abroad.

Overall, however, in the regions around the Mediterranean, the human population more or less continually grew. But much of the birthrate was high through sheer force. With economies dependent on war and slavery, women who were captured and sold after conquests, and their female descendants, had no more right to withhold their bodies, and their fertility, than cows do, and they kept up the supply of slaves in times of peace.

Importantly, though, their fecundity pushed down that of freeborn families. Not only did slaves perform the hardest and most essential jobs, but they also filled many desirable and responsible roles as managers, overseers, artisans, traders, teachers, doctors, and so on. The middling free couple, who lived off a small farm or workshop or a fishing boat or market stall, powerfully preferred to have one son who would inherit the undivided property, in case the divided property provided no livelihood to any of the heirs, and they found themselves competing out in the open marketplace with slaves who got no more than food, shelter, clothing, and a modest allowance in return for their labor. As for daughters, they required substantial dowries, to be paid by their fathers, when they married and joined other families. Having a daughter meant the parents needed to raise and endow their child for another household's benefit.

Hesiod wrote about this state of affairs in the seventh century BCE in his didactic poem *Works and Days*. Hesiod spoke from experience when he wrote that optimally, there should only be *one son*.[1] He had a brother, Perses, with whom he fought over the modest estate the two had inherited, and Hesiod's poem reflects the unrelenting work and care he put into farming his share. Such a farmer might well fall into debt and lose his land (and then perhaps his freedom too, if he had pledged his person as security for a loan, an arrangement that persisted for many centuries in certain parts of the Mediterranean, such as Judea). His *best* prospect after his land was gone was likely as a footloose casual laborer, a rich man's insecure hanger-on, or a mercenary soldier.

Views about family size during antiquity were not hugely different from the current ones in America. The average middle-class couple wonders, "To how many children can we assure a life at least as good as our own? How many college degrees can we afford, if each one costs as much as a modest house?" An essential resource in the face of such questions is family planning, and the need for it was even more stringent in the ancient world, which had a brutal gap between the richest and the poorest, and virtually no social safety net.

"Infant exposure" was the recourse most commonly cited in ancient literature. It is not identical to infanticide, because unwanted babies tended to be left outdoors in fixed, well-known places, and many were picked up and raised as slaves. Rudimentary forms of contraception and abortion were also common, as scores of sources testify. Their use must have been most urgent in the huge urban sex trade, where waiting out a pregnancy would have put a female purveyor out of business for months and turned her body into a mother's. But, barring exceptional circumstances, the calculations would not have been the woman's to make. Most prostitutes were slaves or at least had pimps. In Roman erotic literature, for example, even a well-appointed and cultured "girlfriend," who may at first appear as a free agent, usually turns out to have an exacting manager.

As for married women, they would have preferred—if they could manage it safely, and that was a big if—to prevent or end pregnancies whose hardships and risks could lead only to giving up their newborns to slavery or death. They were not allowed to keep and raise their children if their husband decreed otherwise. But by contrast, the demands on a sex worker and the range of her choices for coping with the reproductive results must have been truly pitiable. She was constantly exposed to conception, and stress could delay menstruation, making it unclear whether she was pregnant or not. She would have needed to dose herself regularly with questionable substances—the silphium plant, perhaps the best option for relatively safe and reliable contraceptive, was in such demand that it went extinct—or face an abortion that risked killing her. How her owner or manager handled her fertility can be left to the imagination, but medical literature from the time leaves hints. One reported technique for dislodging a fetus that would not come away was for two strong men to grasp a woman and shake her violently until her uterus was emptied by force, as if she were a living ketchup bottle.

Even for the best-treated women, there could have been no assurance of receiving safe but effective medications to induce abortions, and surgical techniques were crude. Sometimes, practitioners used not specially adapted instruments but whatever they had on hand—literally so, in what I call uterine fisting: A doctor worked in the womb with a nail fastened to his thumb, dismembering and crushing an expired fetus and cutting through the abdomen from inside to remove the pieces.

Such grisly management of fertility could not have borne the strains of oppressive moralizing. Part of the prevailing deal was that women were not to complain in public, and men were not to pontificate anywhere women would read or hear. Up to the late first century BCE, the extant pronouncements on the rights and wrongs of abortion are almost entirely confined to the cerebral realms of legal, philosophical, and medical literature. Medical literature rarely distinguished clearly between the care for miscarriages and the aftercare of abortions. The concern in either instance is to empty the uterus and prevent bleeding and infection. Assuming that there were many abortions—and medical writers do complain of them—there is no telling how many were induced by doctors themselves. That they quailed before the Hippocratic Oath is nonsense. The Greek text does not forbid abortion in general but merely the use of a "destructive pessary"; a pessary or insert was only one of the available methods of abortion, and it might have been viewed as particularly dangerous to the *woman*. But a more important reason not to credit the oath with deterrent power is that doctors did whatever those who paid them, the heads of families and the owners of slaves, wanted. There were no medical regulatory bodies and no overall control or supervision of daily practice.

Abortion was never outlawed outright or sweepingly in antiquity. And the laws on the books, and the recorded prosecutions, concern the rights of men, not fetuses: A wife must not deprive her husband of a wanted heir or have an abortion to cover up her adultery. For example, around the start of the second century CE, the emperor Septimius Severus decreed the punishment of exile for wives who had abortions because of the crime of depriving their husbands of children. But embarrassment at the thought of dragging the betrayal of their patriarchal authority into the public square would have given many men pause. Prosecutions of either women who had abortions or those who performed them have a mythical quality in their rarity.[2] As for the Hebrew Bible's compendia of laws, there is no trace of a ban on voluntary abortion, only an instruction to punish a miscarriage induced by a violent attacker.[3]

Abortion, moreover, probably wasn't even called abortion wherever it was a routine, discrete recourse. It could have been billed as what American newspaper and magazine ads for abortifacients used to call "menstrual regulation." In any event, the widespread toleration of abortion has an easy explanation: It served men's interests more than women's. Men, not women, determined family size, and they were notably stern about keeping families small. Men, not women, were the usual owners and controllers of prostitutes they wanted to keep working. And of course women, not men, ran the risk of disability or death from the kinds of methods available.

No wonder Greek literature and the first two hundred years of Roman literature contain no trace of antiabortion tub-thumping in the public square, no moral suasion aimed at women or society at large, no religious outcry, no thunderous political rhetoric. Against this background it is astonishing to see antiabortion literature emerging full-grown and fully armed, like Athena out of Zeus's head, in Rome around 18 BCE; and in the genre of love elegy, of all places; and in the unlikeliest of love elegy authors, Ovid.

OVID WAS THE YOUNGEST, MOST PROLIFIC, AND MOST frivolous of the poets cultivated by the first Roman emperor, Augustus, during the so-called Augustan or Golden Age of Latin literature. Ovid had a generally charming persona on paper: witty, self-deprecating, gently hostile to posing pomposity; the speaker is a roué, to be sure, but one who instructs his male audience to pay attention to the clitoris.[4]

The flood of definitely autobiographical poetry he wrote after Augustus banished him to the Black Sea in the year 8 CE leaves us in no doubt about the real man's character and standing. He was a well-to-do, aristocratic Roman who could publicly tout his seemly wife's devotion to the cause of his recall from exile. The playboy life in Rome he depicted in many earlier poems might have been in his past even at the time of writing, or compartmentalized, or wholly imaginary; its cynicism is, at any rate, easy to brush off because in general he so fetchingly hides the grimmer realities of the demimonde under comedy and titillation. Still, Ovid was an Augustan poet, attached to the imperial court. He often inserted tributes—though in his case mostly exaggerated and flippant ones—to the emperor and Rome into his work.

His two "abortion poems" take him where he could not have been comfortable—though, as I'll show, he does a bold and glib job with very unpromising material. Here is the first poem.[5]

> *From the rash ruin of her belly's load,*
> *Corinna languishes, her life in doubt.*
> *Secretly she contrived this monstrous peril;*
> *My rage is just, and yet it yields to fear.*
> *Granted, I got her pregnant—or I think so.*
> *Often I take what might be for what is.*
> *Isis[6] of Paraetonium, Canopus' fields*
> *Of joy, Memphis, and Pharos with its palms,*
> *Where the Nile rushes over its broad basin*
> *Through seven harbors out into the sea:*
> *Your rattles I invoke, Anubis' dread face,*
> *Osirus' fervor in your rites forever,*
> *The snake that slowly slips around your gifts,*
> *And Apis with his horns in your procession;*
> *Turn your face here, and spare two lives in one—*
> *My mistress' and my own—she'll let me live.*
> *Many times at your festivals she served you*
> *With crowds of Cybele's priests in laurel garlands.*
> *And you who pity laboring girls, their swollen*
> *Bodies slow to expel the unseen burden:*

> *Ilithyia,[7] come, and kindly grant my prayer.*
> *She merits life—your gift, if you command it.*
> *Incense I'll offer, white-robed at your altars,*
> *Lay at your feet the promised presents, write,*
> *"Naso[8] gave this, for saving his Corinna."*
> *Only make room: the plaque and gift are coming.*
> *But if, amid great fear, a warning's proper:*
> *Be satisfied with this one clash of arms!*

Nowhere else in Ovid's work, or in any other ancient writing, is there anything like the pair of abortion poems. They affect a first-person, serious, and lengthy engagement with a girlfriend's intimate reproductive crisis. The question of sources—ancient literature tends to be intensely "intertextual," with much of its content and forms borrowed and in effect commenting back and forth between authors and works—is baffling. As I've mentioned, dispassionate and technical commentary dominates extant texts. Literary authors other than Ovid have extremely little to say about abortion.[9] For Ovid's inspiration, it seems requisite to look closer to reality, in his particular social and political contexts.

Though Corinna may be fictional, the existence of the *class* of woman to whom the poem is addressed is as solid as Ovid's own historical identity. The addressee is a professional lover; not a slave, not a slab of flesh displayed nude in a brothel and rented cheap to all comers, but someone aspiring to actual relationships with wealthy men. She may have started life as a slave or come to Rome as a young war captive. Now, anyway, she has become engaging and presentable enough to associate companionably with sophisticated Romans. (Like other romantic female characters in the era's literature, she has a pretentious name, probably a pseudonym: Corinna of Tanagra had been a female Greek lyric poet.) The Roman elegists (Propertius and Tibullus were Ovid's near-contemporaries and fellow protégés of Augustus) berate such a woman and her handlers—again, it is hard to imagine a fully independent courtesan in this society—for greed and cynicism, but in reality her career was short and her income insecure. Shaking down her clients was the logical way to secure her future.

In this social world, pregnancy must have been a true crisis, and a common one: I never read of a male Roman putting himself out to prevent conception.[10] But neither, in ordinary circumstances, could an upper-class Roman marry his pregnant "friend" and raise her child without forfeiting his own position and standing. And to simply guarantee her and the baby long-term maintenance would have been a dicey proposition, setting up a rival household to his regular one. If she could secure such a deal, it likely would not hold, and she risked being abandoned, with no profession and a child—not a citizen, not an heir, and so entitled to nothing—to bring up alone.

The emotional defenses of Ovid's speaker are therefore poignant and convincing. Here is his girlfriend in a helpless, excruciating plight that is largely his fault; therefore in the first poem he undertakes an orgy of self-justification. The second poem, as we will see, has an even more excited presentation, depicting abortion as an incomparable threat to the benign will of the gods for humanity.

Both poems are highly rhetorical, full of elaborate argumentative attacks. The ancient Greeks and Romans were intensely dualistic, habitually riveted on which of two well-matched parties was going to come out ahead. Characteristic and preoccupying communications included speeches in high-stakes lawsuits and debates on vital public policy. Ovid had been trained since childhood to compete in these modes, so on the one occasion in all of his works when he insists absolutely on the male moral high ground, he naturally unleashes an almost blindly one-sided rant.

The trouble is that there is no contest here. The poems are like a driver orating passionately to an unconscious pedestrian he has run down. The speaker, who brought this crisis about by impregnating a vulnerable woman, has all the power, all of the voice, the woman none; but rather than be chastened by the cruelty and absurdity of his own words, he only rants more determinedly. He sounds (if I'm allowed another comparison) very much like a conservative politician in imperialistic America, to which imperialistic Rome is often compared: He demands *everything*, including the appearance of righteousness when he is being a thoughtless brute, and if facts are in the way, he will shout them down.

Granted, there are gestures at sympathy in the two poems. But they are *rhetorical* gestures; they seem to be made only to disarm his contemporary readers, who would likely be shocked that he ventures so officiously into such a sensitive subject at all. In this first poem, the speaker does briefly confront his own responsibility for the pregnancy. Yet, in self-defense, he immediately evokes the literary cliché of the cynical, unfaithful girl and the dupe lover: Perhaps someone else impregnated his girlfriend, and she is making a fool of him. However, he quickly turns away from this unseemly suspicion of a lover who may be dying and spends most of the poem parading his pious anxiety that she not die. Nonetheless, he ends with a threat: The next time Corinna gets pregnant—he seems to presume that there will be a next time—she should not count on winning a "clash of arms," that is, surviving an abortion. By this point she is not, in his telling, a person in a sexual relationship, who tried without any help from her partner to mitigate that relationship's dire consequences; she is willfully at war with her fate and her body and deserves to lose.

But this is not a sharp enough, high-flown enough, momentous enough contrast between good and evil to convince the audience—or the speaker himself, who is used to getting his way. Here is the second abortion poem:

> *What use that girls relax, exempt from war,*
> *Shunning fierce ranks and Amazonian shields,*
> *If, in no battle clash, their own arms wound them?*
> *If they equip blind hands for suicide?*
> *The founder of the ripping out of tender*
> *Fetuses should have died in that same warfare.*
> *So no one points at wrinkles on your belly*
> *A fight awaits you in the cruel arena?*
> *If mothers of old times had chosen this way,*
> *Their trespass would have doomed the human race—*
> *Unless Deucalion redux threw more*
> *Stone seeds of mankind on the empty earth.*[11]
> *Who would have shattered Priam's realm, if Thetis*
> *The sea nymph hadn't borne her lawful burden?*[12]
> *In her twin-swollen belly, Ilia*
> *Would have brought lordly Rome down, with its founder.*[13]
> *Had Venus trespassed on unborn Aeneas,*
> *It would have meant a world bereft of Caesars.*[14]
> *You would have perished, not been born so lovely,*
> *Had this, your undertaking, been your mother's.*
> *And me—saved for a better fate, to die*
> *For love—my mother could have kept from daylight.*

Why cheat the vine of growing grapes, why pluck
The bitter, early fruit with your cruel hand?
Let what is ripe flow forth, what's started grow:
Life is a prize that's worth a short delay.
Why do you thrust in spears and dig your guts out,
Give deadly drugs to people not yet born?
Medea's blamed, when splashed with her sons' blood.[15]
Itys, slain by his mother, is lamented.[16]
Both were cruel parents, but had tragic reasons,
And with their kindred blood paid back their husbands.
What Tereus, what Jason goads you, tell me,
To take a jittery hand to your own bodies?
Tigresses in Armenian lairs don't do this.
No lioness would dare destroy her young.
But young girls do—not that they get off lightly.
They often die from their internal slaughter—
Die, and are carried, loose-haired, to the pyre,
And anyone who sees cries out, "She earned it!"
Let what I've said, though, melt in lofty breezes,
Let everything I've augured have no force.
Kind gods, grant safety in this single sin.
Enough! But punish any further guilt.

Ovid, in his increasingly sweeping, high-pitched rhetoric, has all but abandoned his original addressee, Corinna, as an individual; he no longer uses his lover's name, nor does he depict any longer his self-righteous fear over the danger she has placed herself in and his efforts to bring her ritual aid. He now offers nothing in a truly personal vein except a couple of rhetorical sallies, adapted from the clichés of being born beautiful and of dying for love: She would not have been born beautiful had she been aborted, and he would not have died for love had he been aborted. His main rhetorical task here is to accuse "girls" of both committing suicide and placing divine history and the civilized world at risk for fear of wrinkles on their bellies—no other motivation for abortion is cited.[17]

For an author with such elaborate pretensions to being inside women's heads, the cold vilification of his second abortion poem is shocking. Near the end, women who die from abortions are actually shown going to their pyres amid a chorus of "serves her right!"—though we have no other evidence of such scenarios in the ancient world. And this time when the speaker warns his girlfriend against a second abortion, he openly plans to side with the divine tribunal if she reoffends.

To sustain such rage against substantially helpless people Ovid uses the kind of towering unreason that informs American antiabortion politics. It is commonly said today that certain women find themselves with unwanted pregnancies because of their irresponsibility, which also causes them to seek abortions; but the very same women, it is said, can also save society from collapse and implement the divine plan for the future by becoming mothers. Those who in fact have little choice in whether or not to become pregnant, and cannot imagine how they will care for a single baby, are supposed to be able to save the world with only a little inconvenience.

Ovid makes his point with several *exempla* or proof texts (not from the Bible in his case, of course, but from pagan mythology) about the momentous importance of seeing an unwanted pregnancy through. The most popular American antiabortion exemplum is the Virgin Mary's pregnancy: What would have happened to the world had she thought only of herself and aborted Jesus? Ovid provides several proof texts along similar lines, first by citing three famous role models who suffered greatly in producing providential offspring; their offspring, in their turn, suffered in continuing to fulfil a long-term and (to them) mysterious providence.

The first role model is Thetis, a goddess married by force to the mortal Peleus (he consummates the marriage with a divinely assisted rape), a deliberate move to keep her from producing too powerful a being as a son. The *Iliad* shows her years later, full of grief because she cannot protect her half-mortal child Achilles from an early death on the battlefield. Second, Rhea Silvia, also known as Ilia, was a Vestal Virgin raped by the god Mars and punished for her pregnancy. Slated for death, her twin infants are secretly rescued and grow up as shepherds. After their royal bloodline is eventually revealed, one murders the other in response to his competitive taunts. And third, the goddess Venus falls under a vengeful enchantment, seduces the mortal Anchises, and gives birth to Aeneas. Nymphs raise the baby in secret because his mother is dismayed and humiliated by his origin. In Vergil's telling, she intervenes magically to help him as an adult in his torturous quest for an Italian kingdom, but he protests bitterly against her very occasional, teasing, and withholding presence.

The summaries of these myths read like a little anthology of minimally sanitized stories inspired by real-life rationales for terminating a pregnancy. But Ovid has carefully selected tales framed by religious and patriotic awe. Each relates to Vergil's blockbuster patriotic epic the *Aeneid*, probably recently published, and if not, then known in outline and excitedly awaited. Fate, divine pronouncements, and prophesies decree the intertwined absolutes of history in all these cases. Achilles must be born in order to kill Troy's defender Hector so that the city falls and its surviving prince Aeneas—who must of course first be born—goes as a refugee to Italy to found the Roman nation and the Julian bloodline, which will culminate in the first and current Roman emperor Augustus, peacemaker after decades of civil wars, ruler and Romanizer of most of the known world. In the meantime, Ilia must give birth to Romulus, who will found Rome, which is destined to one day appoint Augustus as a god.

In purported parallel, Ovid presents a negative pair of exempla, cases of child murder in myth (the children are old enough to know that their mothers are killing them) that are supposed to deter women from abortion: They don't want to be like these unnatural, vicious mothers, do they? Women who have abortions, it's implied, are worse than the animal mothers the speaker goes on to cite, who do not kill their young.[18] This ties in with what Ovid urges earlier in the poem, associating women with agricultural production, the basis of traditional metaphors for sex and childbearing. Women are like land or crops to be cultivated (a Latin term for the penis is *vomer* or "ploughshare") or animals to be tamed, worked, and bred. Unlike the wild animal mothers who do not destroy their young, women who have abortions are unnatural, distorted, frustrating the productive, world-sustaining purpose for which they were created.

American conservatives cherish natural law arguments and have often applied them in the antiabortion crusade. Catholic and Evangelical scholarly pundits are fond of asserting what the human *natura* (essence) and *telos* (proper purpose) are: heterosexual, nuclear-family domestic or else celibate, wholesomely erotic only in connection to reproduction, unquestioningly subservient to a clerical hierarchy's representation of the divine will.

The ancient philosophers from whom the basic terms are drawn would have choked on their cheese to hear them being deployed in this way.

It is more and more apparent that concepts of natural law are extremely problematic in connection to human reproduction. Neither natural science nor a workable legal system can support them. In this respect, antiabortion politics are not like other reform movements. Africans were not, according to any sustainable logic or evidence, created for white exploitation, so whites couldn't indefinitely get away with pretending they were, any more than men could get away with pretending that women were by nature too weak-minded to vote. It is, above all, a clear moral hazard to allow human beings to be defined as to their essence and purpose by those intent on controlling and exploiting them.

Even if this were not the case, mere assertions of what is "natural" tend to be reductive to the point of uselessness. The natural "right to life" of a fetus as posited by modern thinkers, like Ovid's invocation of the rightness of a fetus developing and being born, in parallel to the rightness of fruit growing and being harvested, is just a platitude and a sanctity, with no respect for the complexity of the real world in which (for example) a crop with a contagious blight or a nonviable fetus endangering the mother's life might need to be destroyed. Romans worshipped agriculture—Ovid's contemporary Vergil had written that farming made Rome "the most beautiful thing on earth"[19]—as Americans worship the Declaration of Independence, which enshrines "life" among "inalienable" rights, and the Constitution, which has expanded rights through a series of amendments and so might be amended to protect human life "from the moment of conception." Ovid is, similarly to right-wing Americans, reaching into general cultural sanctities rather than making a logical argument or affirming a salient reality.

As a demonstration of barbarity contrasting with Roman civilization, in which nature and culture are supposed to combine to vindicate divine providence, Ovid gives two examples of behavior native to lawless lands. One example involves King Tereus of Thrace, who rapes his young Athenian sister-in-law Philomela, imprisons her, and cuts her tongue out to prevent her witness against him. His wife Procne finds out, kills their son, and serves him up to the wrongdoer in the classic fricassee. Then a divinity turns the king and the two women into birds, as if clubbing all the noisy kids with the same broomstick in the time-honored manner. In the second example, Medea, a princess of Colchis on the Black Sea, has saved the young Jason from her murderous father, then married him and had two sons. She now kills the brothers after Jason arranges to abandon her in favor of an advantageous new union; she kills the prospective bride and father-in-law for good measure. She escapes on a magic chariot, her powerful curses lording it over her husband's weak ones.

But weirdly, in Ovid's grand, hysterical scheme, these infanticides come across as lesser crimes. Procne and Medea kill their children out of rage when they are horribly provoked; it is cruel of them, but to a degree understandable, and the consequences do not reverberate down history. But what Thetis, Ilia, and Venus were putatively tempted to do was something hugely atrocious, genocidal rather than murderous, something we might compare with starting a nuclear exchange. The abortions they might have had would have knocked the world off its axis and frustrated the gods' benign will for all of humanity. Abortion is thus depicted as the ultimate crime, exponentially worse than killing your little boy and feeding him to his father, or killing your two little boys and displaying their bodies to their father with words of hatred and contempt.

What is more, the rhetoric seeks to dissolve the difference between the abortion of semidivine fetuses who would be born to further the divinely decreed destiny of Rome, and the abortion of sex-workers' fetuses who would be born outside of patriarchal homes and face very uncertain prospects. Ovid's judgment is blindingly sweeping, if not ridiculous, a fitting ancestor to modern religious conservatives' billing of abortion as the super-crime, a crime like genocide (to which in fact it is often explicitly compared), a crime for which no plea of necessity (which applies when an individual commits a criminal act in order to prevent a greater harm from happening) can ever be admitted.[20]

How did Ovid, who liked to show himself as the conquered captive and slave of erotic love, concoct such harsh and absolutist notions about ordinary results of sex, pregnancy, and abortion? Was it the result merely of his—or his persona's—fast-talking guilt and eagerness to avoid responsibility, or were there special historical reasons behind this first extant instance of antiabortion propaganda, set as it is against a background of general, pragmatic, paternalistic tolerance of abortion?

OCTAVIAN SECURED HIS POSITION AT THE HEAD OF THE Roman empire in 31 BCE after victory in a lengthy civil war, the last of a fairly tight sequence of Roman civil wars stretching back more than half a century. Augustus was the honorific title he gave himself, a made-up name that to Latin speakers would have suggested prophetic power and general authority, as well as the blessing and prosperity he claimed his reign offered. He was arguably the first modern autocrat, presiding over a careful semblance of the old participatory polity, the Republic, like a banana republic's "president" who is "chosen" time after time in sham elections. Augustus likewise achieved substantial hegemony without admitting that he was doing so, and his power seems to have been greater for being less explicit. He could work established systems (violently when he thought necessary), often through proxies who held traditional offices, and at the same time create craven, self-betraying loyalty among his subjects by compelling them to lie about what was happening.

For example, parts of inheritances were customarily an important medium of exchange in public life. To pay an orator to defend you in court or prosecute your enemies was forbidden by law, but legal advocacy was among the many favors for which a codicil to a will could be compensation: You could just write your lawyer in for a small percentage. Augustus made it known that, as the whole nation's benign patron, he constantly did *everybody* favors; hence he expected that a portion of every estate would go to him. People with property quickly fell in with this expectation and bequeathed the emperor a share. They knew that if they didn't, he could plunder everything from their bereaved families. He may have ended up the richest man in the history of the world.

Augustus likewise insinuated himself into Roman culture like a wolf into a sheep's toga. Rome had engendered a mostly unremarkable array of art, architecture, and literature. Besides making imperial urban landscapes a virtual image of himself, Augustus commissioned writers and artists to produce striking propaganda. He cultivated a uniquely talented and influential group of authors, including Vergil, Horace, and Livy, whom he directed to advertise the heavenly mission of the Roman race—to be led from now on by Augustus and his heirs—to subdue and rule the world in its own best interest.

Augustus boasted with an ambition previously unknown except in the god-kings of Egypt and the Near East; but unlike them, he wielded genuinely popular literature. It was far superior in quality to what had been available in Latin a generation before, and he left the authors free to develop their own aesthetics and spend most of their time on subject matter that interested them personally. This way it appeared to the Roman readership as if intellectuals were glorifying Augustus spontaneously and voluntarily. This is how Vergil got to write pastoral sketches, Horace drinking songs, and Ovid love poetry, all three of them refining Latin verse forms for which Romans were hungry; before this, the Greeks had had nearly all the literary glory. In a similar way, Stalin and Hitler recognized the need to win over discerning viewers with the imported mode of film that had achieved so much elsewhere, and they gave their leading film directors the resources and latitude they needed to create works that tapped into their own ideas of what would appeal, resulting in productions that, at least in their forms, are still impressive.

But Ovid's favorite topic, seduction, would eventually help get him into serious trouble. He himself cites his *Art of Love* (which celebrated the demimonde as if the empire existed only to supply enticing "girls" from conquered nations) and some still-unidentified "mistake"[21] as the causes of his exile in 8 CE to an imperial outpost on the Black Sea, where he remained until his death around ten years later. But what does this have to do with the abortion poems, which were part of his *Amores*, not his *Art of Love*, and which were not, apparently, in the dock for his exile?

In 18 and 17 BCE, Ovid was very likely working on some of the later of his five books of *Amores* (eventually edited down to three), a work published as a whole in 16 or 15 BCE; the abortion poems appear in what is now Book 2. The impression the poet had given to Augustus (who liked to hear everything he funded recited as soon as it was written) years earlier with the introductory poems of Book 1 could not have been wholly to the powerful patron's taste. These important "programmatic" compositions not only show love affairs as an absorbing, highly civilized counterworld to the official and dutiful version of Roman life, but also deal some sharp jabs at the puffery of Roman imperial power. In *Amores* 1.2, Ovid actually spoofs the Roman military triumph procession, an immense and glorious celebration including a display of foreign captives, as a means to display his own subjection and enslavement by the love god, Cupid. But Augustus was one to project geniality and tolerance when he was first vexed and save a yank of the chain for the right moment. I think that for Ovid a yank came in the year 18 or 17 BCE and was in the direction of fertility propaganda.

As it happened, during the years 18 and 17 Augustus promulgated the first items of what historians call his "moral legislation." What better way to punish this court poet who advertised himself as a playboy than to force him to tout righteous, self-sacrificial fertility in the cause of Rome's high destiny? If the poems stuck in Ovid's stylus, if they were the most uncongenial works he had ever written, if he had to whip himself into weird poses of high dudgeon just to get through them, then so much the better. Augustus didn't introduce his program for the reform of women and family life because people were going to like it; they had better learn from his chief proponent of good times himself about their patriotic duty to reproduce.

An aim of the harsh new laws, however, was *legitimate* birth, so Ovid's topical awkwardness would have been particularly acute. Augustus set out to curb adultery (to the Romans, this meant any extramarital sex for wives, but for men only sex with married women) and to mandate marriage and childbearing, taking a stride toward totalitarianism by trying to place citizens' most intimate matters under state control. In support of the legislation, the emperor argued on a practical level what the second poem argues in sweeping mythical and historical terms: Those who placed their own selfish interests above the imperative of childbearing would be the doom of Rome.

"Family values" is a questionable term at best; it is wildly unsuited to Augustus's program. Since prehistoric times, each Roman home had acted as a small kingdom. But, though the rule of the paterfamilias was theoretically almost absolute, his interest in maintaining workable relationships inside and outside his walls, and in shining up the reputation of everyone who belonged to him, made him often lenient and flexible in practice. The new legislation, to an extent previously unknown in the Greek and Roman world—except for a few generations in the barracks commonwealth of Sparta—sought to break personal ties and forcefully redirect loyalty away from the household head to the state.

The reforms took special aim at fertile women in their accustomed place at the intimate center of families. Augustus in effect decreed that he was shifting women's sexual and reproductive behavior from under the weak supervision of fathers and husbands. He was applying the state's stern but benevolent remedies to rampant, civilization-threatening depravity—the pursuit of mere sexual kicks on the part of people who should be turning out the copious, well-cared-for next generation of the citizenry.

To do this, Augustus sought to turn family members against each other by force and make impressive deterrent examples of those who strayed. Fathers were in some cases permitted to kill their adulterous daughters and their lovers, and husbands were to divorce their adulterous wives or be prosecuted as pimps. The hardship and breakup of families were to be ensured by the distant exile of the culprits as well as brutal financial penalties.

As for mandated marriage and childbearing, Augustus in effect maneuvered legislatively to weaken or eliminate clans who were not self-sacrificially loyal to him, right down to the use of their marriage beds. Extended families of any substance and security maintained themselves through inheritance—which brings us back to Augustus's interference with that custom; but in the moral legislation he was attempting a more extensive, more destructive interference in it.

Livelihoods were passed down through the generations in the form of material goods, which were characteristically fixed-investment businesses (farms, craft workshops, shipping companies, tenement rentals, and so on) and the rural estates to which the owners could retreat during hard times, if they were urbanites. Small chips of this accumulated wealth could go out of the family to pay for past favors, and a sizable chip had to go to the emperor, but family stability depended on keeping the wealth substantially undiminished.

Protecting inheritance over generations entailed an array of traditional practices, including careful negotiation and decision-making about family formation. For example, it was common to hold a son back from marrying—he needed his father's permission, as he did for every other step—until he was thirty or even older, to ensure that he was far enough developed as a community member to head a nuclear family and, on this basis, prepare for legal and financial independence, which technically didn't come about until his father died. His late marriage would also mean fewer pregnancies to deal with in the quest for a suitably small number of surviving children. Delaying marriage also gave his older relatives time to secure the right mate for him (attractive, healthy, well brought up, belonging to a family that could offer the largest dowry and the best economic, social, or political alliance); they might need to wait until she became available through pubescence, divorce, or widowhood.

Through his legislation, Augustus tied the right to inherit to early marriage (men were not to wait past the age of twenty-five), prompt remarriage, and regular breeding. To meet these requirements, citizens would have to forego most or all contraception and abortion, and to raise most or all of the legitimate children born. In other words, Augustus moved to take away the main means by which families regulated and sustained themselves: controlling their size at their own convenience and according to their means. So much for family-friendly policy.

There is no evidence that Augustus had any sincere concern for the moral integrity or the viable size of the Roman population. Rather than suffering a demographic crisis, Rome and its domains were populous, prosperous, and politically stable like never before. It is hard to gauge whether ethnic Romans were cutting back on childbearing, but they had never been prolific, and it might even have been that in this time of peace and material comfort, after the civil wars that had reached all over their known world, they were having more babies, like Americans after World War II.

In any case, Romans were well able to fill economic and social gaps caused by changing demography: slavery, class and professional mobility, cultural assimilation and immigration,[22] and technological innovation, all of which were booming during the early empire. Augustus, one of the savviest politicians in history, knew all this. He could not have feared that Roman civilization was going to implode because of a low birthrate. Like many of the right-wing American politicians claiming that the use of abortion and contraception will be the doom of America, Augustus had other reasons for his pro-marriage and pro-natal measures.

Augustus's moral legislation was mainly a power move against his old enemies, the independent-minded Roman elite—senators, knights (a wealthy commercial class), bankers, military commanders, and high-level public administrators—who had fought him in the civil wars, after assassinating his great-uncle Julius Caesar. Year after year following Augustus's decisive military victory and initial unconstitutional power grabs, they had tried to block his ambitions for complete power and a dynasty that could never be dislodged. If Augustus had any concern in pushing through his "reforms," it was a willed and self-serving one. What he *could* hope to achieve was a campaign of harassment and terror that might loosen the networks that held out against him, networks in which families were the ropes, intermarriage the knots, and a household's far-reaching legal autonomy and inherited wealth the supporting scaffolding. Even if he couldn't shake that structure, he could still depict the whole class of his political opponents as wicked, decadent, and unfit to govern because of what they did in their private lives. The campaign is somewhat similar to the one waged against liberal America in the name of "unborn life"; it falls short of forcing such people to change their views and their behavior, but its propaganda success and hence its electoral influence have been stunning.

These new laws also provided Augustus with handy scapegoating tactics for addressing—or rather, for trying to dodge—an acute public opinion problem for his new regime. The most recent series of Roman civil wars, which had ended with Augustus's rise to sole power, was notorious for its folly and brutality. These wars happened for the basic reason that the Republic's oligarchs did not have the decency and restraint to divide up more fairly—or at least less violently—the huge influx of wealth from foreign conquests that spread over the map. The result was the nearest thing to date to world war, with the breakdown of existing rules of war and other civilized norms as the stakes increased.

The lingering trouble for Augustus was that he had been a relentless partisan in this struggle from his teens, a fitting heir (he was literally the adoptive son) of the notorious dictator and general Julius Caesar, who, for example, had matter-of-factly cut off the hands of all the military-age males in the conquered Gaulish city of Uxellodunum to prevent future resistance. The civil wars lingered in public memory—they were widely and openly deplored—and Augustus shared the taint of blood-lust, power-hunger, and fratricide.[23] It was convenient, as it always is, to lay the fate of a nation distractingly at women's door, especially after a monumental fiasco like prolonged and very bloody warfare.[24] Augustus, a master of the propagandistic gesture, crowned his misogyny with the majesty of law.

And, through his literary minion, he seems to have crowned the new laws with a particularly obnoxious piece of misogynist misdirection, a women-blaming allusion to civil war itself. Ovid, in the course of his wild-sounding protests that the mere possibility of abortion puts the very existence of Rome in peril, cites the story of Romulus and Remus, which was generally used to illustrate Rome's original sin of fratricidal civil strife: The twin founders of Rome couldn't get along when they had nothing to fight over but rival "city walls" that were rows of rocks stacked up a foot or so high. According to Ovid, the threat to the nation and the world is not the way male leaders behave, it is that we can imagine the leaders' mothers aborting them. Abortion is thus set up hopefully to be the distractor par excellence, and women with their capacity for reproductive choice to be the ultimate scapegoats. This has also happened, and to great electoral effect, in conservative segments of twentieth- and twenty-first-century America, where many howling past wrongs and urgent public-policy needs take a back seat to the alleged "holocaust of the unborn."

It is hard, of course, to tell to what extent Augustus's particular woman-blaming propaganda dodges worked for him in practice. They certainly didn't work to the extent of persuading Romans to change their habits of family formation. Romans disliked and evaded the new morality legislation with special energy where this part of their lives was concerned. Sham marriages in a pinch (when an inheritance was pending, for example); adoption rituals for show; and paper betrothals to girls many years under puberty were among the dodges targeted by equally ineffective laws far down the imperial road.

But as with leaders of the American antiabortion movement, no embarrassment, no frustration, no pressure, no force of facts could make Augustus get off this political hobby horse and find another. When a crowd of knights petitioned him for relief from his already modified but still oppressive laws on family life, he dandled some of the children of his popular young relative Germanicus in his lap, and had Germanicus dandle others, and conveyed to his audience that this tableau was all the answer they were going to get.

There is, by the way, a bitter irony in the story of the emperor posing with Germanicus's children (there were six surviving ones), the pride of his budding dynasty, to shame Roman citizens who were begging to be spared the burdens of large families. The issue was not only that he could afford one and they couldn't; there also loomed the ugly thing that Hesiod had written of six centuries before: fighting over the patrimony among more than one claimant. The question of the imperial succession was in fact already shaping into gory dynastic intrigue. In time, news of rivalrous poisonings and violent murders seeped from the palace with what must have been sickening regularity. The children on Augustus's lap probably included Caligula, who grew up to be a rumored expert at clearing the crowded field for himself.

But very likely those in the audience were not speculating about the future of Germanicus's family, or about the future of any families but their own. That is the great challenge to any large institution that wants to suddenly dictate whether people should have more children or fewer. The will to procreate is part of the self, part of the will to survive and belong and prosper; it is very hard to interfere with from on high. This is why the most ingenious Augustan poet, Ovid, flailed with rather desperate-sounding ingenuity for a persuasive reason that courtesans should refrain from abortions for the good of Roman civilization and could come up only with a feral, childishly factitious rant that probably impressed no one. This is why his patron, the most powerful man on earth, could not arrange suitable propaganda for his enduring pet project.

But as ideas and culture shifted, there would be other attempts at changing people's reproductive behavior from what they chose in their own interest—attempts that would be progressively more successful, and progressively more destructive.

CHAPTER 2

PREGNANT AND FOOT-WASHING AND IN THE KITCHEN

Early Christian Reproductive Backlash

IN THE SECOND-CENTURY CE ROMAN EMPIRE, RELATIVE peace, prosperity, and political stability offered married women the usual advantages. They were more active in the economy and the culture at large than before, more sociable yet more self-reliant in their thinking, and less restricted by their families. As what we might (loosely) call middle-class status spread to a greater number of families, more could afford the services of a wet nurse or nanny (normally the same person, a slave or a free woman who took on this work as a trade).

The circulation of Juvenal's *Satire 6*—a long poem that is a misogynist classic—from around the start of the second century is not a contradiction but a confirmation of this happier, freer scene for wives. *Satire 6* formed part of the pagan Roman backlash against such women, who had been piling up their socioeconomic gains throughout the first century CE and more or less ignoring the Augustan morality legislation meant to control and restrict them. As Susan Faludi documents in the case of America in her 1991 book *Backlash*, an angry reaction can follow gains in women's rights and freedoms, and this was Juvenal's issue. But the poet's smolderingly frustrated voice and the alleged outrages he parades serve to confirm not only how far women had come, but how little men could do about it.

Juvenal depicts a woman who insists on discussing current affairs with men in public; a woman who enjoys the sport of fencing; and women who have male and female lovers, travel (even helping sailors with the ship's rigging), and take part in an exclusively female "religious" gathering that turns into a bawdy dance party and then an orgy. Regarding family formation, however, Juvenal strikes notes that are distinctly less shrill, and even similar to modern liberal talking points: Rich women have access to medical resources and clandestine adoptions that allow them to give birth rarely; poor women have no choice but to undergo the dangers of childbirth and the work of infant care.[1] Fiercely generalizing *reproductive* misogyny seems to have been a bridge too far even for Juvenal, the most ornery of pagan Roman woman-haters.

At any rate, Roman women did not take the backlash best represented by Juvenal lying down. Though their household power was still less than they might wish, and their political activities extremely limited, they certainly had their own forms of communication to fight against misogynist propaganda. Mediterranean peoples had outdoor, public cultures, and a woman's mere stroll down the street could advertise her as an important person. Apuleius's cosmopolitan Latin novel *The Golden Ass*, probably written around 150 CE, introduces a wife in the center of her household's entourage as a reservoir of its prestige and the director of its generous and cultured hospitality. Exploring a strange city on his first morning there, the young protagonist Lucius sees a richly dressed woman walking beside her husband, servants accompanying them. The husband is delighted to recognize Lucius and urges him to greet the woman, but the young man hangs back, blushing and looking down, because he doesn't think he knows her.

> Now she turned and gazed at me. "Look at him! He knows just how to behave—you can tell what a good family he's from. He gets his modesty from that faultless mother of his. And, upon my life, he looks exactly like her. He's tall but not too tall, slender but still juicy, and just rosy enough. He doesn't wear that blond hair of his like a sissy. His eyes are quite a light blue, but they're wide-awake and glittering like an eagle's. His whole face is just a flower. He walks nicely but doesn't mince.
>
> "I cared for you with these hands, Lucius," she continued. "How could I not have? I'm not only your mother's relative; we were reared together. Both of us descend from the family of Plutarch, we suckled from the same nurse at the same time, and we grew up with a bond like sisterhood. It's only our rank that's different now, because she married a great statesman, while my marriage keeps me in private life. I'm Byrrhena! I'm sure the people who reared you mentioned me often—don't you remember? Don't hang back but come

and accept my hospitality; there shouldn't be any difference between my home and yours."²

Apuleius's novel is not interested in whether Byrrhena has any children; her standing does not depend on motherhood. She has been a second mother to Lucius, but now she evaluates him in lubricious tones, though without tainting her kindness, sagacity, or innocent egotism; in fact, she offers him excellent advice as the story goes forward. She very likely represents a real-life type of upper-class women, one whose status was growing in parallel to their business and property rights.

The Golden Ass is a pagan book. Christianity, after its initial wave of evangelism in the first century, had no room for such expansive, indulgent treatment of women. In Christian communities, women were commanded and shamed, as an entire class, into extreme self-abnegation. The only Christian heroines were martyrs, glorified for volunteering for death, the utterances of nearly all limited to declaring their faith, affirming their willingness to die, and remarking on what a privilege it was to do so. Theologians had to work out a twisted excuse for glorifying such women at all: They must not be regarded as women, who were cursed and degraded by Eve's crimes of disobeying God, and inducing Adam to disobey along with her, so that sin, suffering, and death would be the lot of all their descendants. Through women martyrs' self-sacrifice, they were magically infused with the pure, exalted, *masculine* divine essence.

While pagan women were carving out greater opportunity with little interference, Christian wives were urged downward into dark confinement, gratuitously penitential frumpery, and other humiliations driven by male spite. Some of the Church

Fathers waxed hysterical on the subject of finery and grooming, as if a pair of lapis earrings and an up-do under a gauzy veil really shocked their conscience.[3] Christianity's first literary superstar, Tertullian, who wrote during the late second and early third centuries, enshrined this sentiment with an entire treatise against female ornamentation, *On the Apparel of Women*. Perhaps not coincidentally, he was also the first author to clearly state an absolutist position on abortion: It is no different from infanticide, and he does not grant that a very early stage of pregnancy is an extenuation.[4] The Catholic Church did not make firm and lasting decrees in this direction until much later.[5]

Tertullian's strictures against beautification were not merely motivated by displeasure at female vanity. They were part of much more substantial assaults that Christianity made on women's integrity. The Church Father Jerome (c. 345–420) leaned on heiresses to make vows of chastity, remain childless, and gift the church the estates that children would have inherited, with the apparent idea that these women's lives and possessions should be under the church's control and for its use. The idea came to be expressed also through the requirement that the church sanctify marriages,[6] through the bans on women owning or managing property, and in other laws such as the ones regulating—but not forbidding—the beating of wives. Pagan Roman law, as well as pagan Roman culture in general, had been comparatively woman-friendly.

In this context, baubles had an outsize significance for Christians. The pagan Apuleius pointedly identifies Byrrhena's rich outfit as a sign of marriage. Along with her escort, the accoutrements are part of her forcefield in public, which makes the young man afraid to speak to her even when she speaks to him first.

Women of much lower station—including street-walkers, distinguishable from married women and respectable virgins by their more revealing clothing—also benefitted from the logic of dressing better than they could have afforded on their own: There was male muscle behind even modest finery. A woman who wasn't at all soigné, who didn't have a clean tunic or a string of glass beads to go out in, would be the object of troublesome interest everywhere she went, the assumption being that she had no protection and was literally up for grabs.

Such a heightened threat of harassment or worse was useful to the Christian authorities in one way. Men who deprived women of their virtual armor of nice things, and in fact imposed a sort of Christian uniform—special, very plain and cheap attire and hairstyling that labeled them as members of this vulnerable group—made it more dangerous for them to go out. The prescribed female look not only humbled Christian women but helped keep them isolated and confined, without options beyond serving their men uncomplainingly.

That this is exactly what the Christian hierarchy wanted is first evidenced in the Pastoral Epistles of the New Testament: 1 and 2 Timothy and Titus. These short treatises in the form of letters were likely written in the early second century and were falsely ascribed to Paul, who had died in the '60s of the previous century. The letters set out rationales for a shattering-looking crackdown. Not even notoriously restrictive Classical Athens, with its deep paranoia about female adultery, made more drastic efforts to try to repress and control women. Athenian men recognized, for example, that young wives confined in the alien, often hostile environment of their husbands' family homes would break down if they could never relax and blow off steam, so they were permitted to visit friends and relatives and attend all-female festivities.

Christian women, according to the Pastoral Epistles, were not supposed to visit one another or converse together in private at all. Athenian women's childbearing and childrearing obligations were limited by a tradition of small families and their husbands' inability to provide for larger ones. Christian women were told that their salvation, their only chance at immortal life, depended on childbearing. With this incentive (and threat) among the causes, their fertility might well have risen in spite of Christians' generally greater poverty.[7]

In any event, the Pastoral Epistles' "salvation through childbearing" decree is the earliest known of many Christian efforts to take fertility decisions out of couples' hands and make childbearing a religious obligation, inarguable and subject to no practicalities. We can see little of the beginning of the campaign because of the obscurity, even secrecy, in which the predominantly lower-class and sometimes persecuted early Christians lived, but over time the idea of holy fertility would have rather stunning results, including the American Quiverfull movement, named from Psalms 127:3–5, a passage that extolls children as "a heritage from the Lord," like arrows filling a quiver. This movement treats fertility less like a religious witness and more like a controlling way of life, an option that takes other important options—school for the children, for example—off the table.

The Quiverfull movement is an extreme development, but where the treatment of women is concerned, there are broad similarities between the first Christian pro-fertility regimen we can glimpse here through the New Testament and the latest ones flourishing in far-right America. Most glaring is the isolation and degradation of women, to make them usable at will for childbearing and the most menial tasks of childcare and the household: The guidance of the children and the shaping of their minds is supposed to be up to men, and it is delegated to women only if they carry it out by rote.

Quite striking restrictions on women, which must have been isolating and degrading in their effect if not their conscious purpose, are already in evidence in Christian antiquity. One of these restrictions concerns bathing. Under the Roman Empire, every sizable town had a bathhouse, and, by a common arrangement, women alone had the right to visit it during a certain time of day, usually the morning. Apuleius shows that even if a pagan woman had a jealous husband who would have liked to lock her up all the time, her regular trips to the baths were nonnegotiable, no less when he was out of town than when he was at home.[8] Women were thus entitled to exercise together, exchange news, and bathe in a public place that was temporarily cleared of men—no trivial release in their generally dull and narrow lives. The Church Fathers, however, strongly disapproved of women going to bathhouses, and the author of the Pastoral Epistles may have had these places in mind when he forbade women to gather and talk. But very few homes, and fewer Christian ones (because, again, they were on average poorer), had private bathing facilities other than jars and basins and a cauldron for heating water with expensive wood or charcoal; most Christian women avoiding the public baths would have lacked even the convenient and comfortable means to stay clean.

In Roman culture, cleanliness meant far more than hygiene. *Lautus*, most literally "washed," was used to refer to someone tasteful and refined, suitable for other people's senses and thus for social life; in Roman literature, the physical opposite of *lautus* is "reeking like a goat." *Mundus*, most literally "cleanly" or "neat," also meant "fine" or "proper," even in the moral sense. The words applied even-handedly to men and women who had the benefits of urban cultivation. The person who could not bathe thoroughly but only dab and could not even wear clothes that were expertly dyed or bleached outside the home would have felt like an outcast. Slaves of average privilege went to public baths and dressed up on occasion. They were even allowed to participate in lighthearted social activities. Christian women would have been considered, in these respects, beneath the status of ordinary pagan slaves.

But in the Pastoral Epistles, the zinger of woman-targeting is penitential childbearing. It is the crescendo of a key passage about the perniciousness of women. Here is the passage in 1 Timothy 2; I include the segue from the letter's generalizing and authority-establishing opening:

> 5 For there is one God, and there is one mediator between God and human beings, the human being Jesus the Anointed One, 6 who gave himself as a ransom for everyone—the testimony to this coming at the proper times.
>
> 7 For this purpose I was appointed as a herald and an envoy—I speak the truth, I am not lying—a teacher of the non-Jews in faith and truth.
>
> 8 Therefore I want the men everywhere to pray, lifting up pure and holy hands, without anger or dispute.
>
> 9 In the same way, I want the women to dress in an appropriate manner, with modesty and self-control, not with their hair woven together, or gold or pearls or expensive clothing, 10 but with good deeds, as becomes women who claim to worship God.

> 11 A woman is to learn in quietude and full subordination. 12 I do not permit a woman to teach, or to dictate to a man; she is instead to remain in quietude. 13 For Adam was molded first, and then Eve. 14 And it was not Adam who was tricked; rather, the woman was thoroughly tricked and became a wrongdoer. 15 But a woman will be saved through childbearing, if they continue in faith and love and pure holiness, with self-control.[9]

Verse 6's "everyone," meaning all humankind, saved through Jesus's sacrifice, is discarded within two verses. It is first stated that the men (the rare gender-emphatic word *andres* is used) simply need to pray, expressing their faith in Jesus, but the women are to bear children—and behave perfectly—in order to be saved. The author cites the story of Adam and Eve as the reason for this rewriting of basic Christian theology. Genesis states in one creation story—the second of two—that part of woman's eternal punishment for Eve's disobedience to God is to have a husband who will rule over her. But she is not the only dupe of the serpent in the biblical tale, and not the only condemned and punished sinner to come out of Eden. God punishes the snake first and most severely, and the human pair together and partly in parallel to one another. While the woman is subordinated, both are exiled from the garden; the man will sweat for food, and childbirth will become painful.

For a Christian author to make childbearing in itself a woman's main penance was bizarre, and not only because this helps turn basic Christian beliefs about sin and salvation inside out and upside down. Perilous and painful as birth was in the ancient world, motherhood was the dutiful glory of married women, a way for them to raise their status unassailably—which marriage alone would not do. This is particularly evident in Jewish scripture, in which wives pine for fertility and revel when blessed with it; they then stand for the future of their people, whom God will not abandon to desolation in spite of their collective mistakes and troubles. The stories of the nativity in the Gospels of Matthew and Luke (writings that date from the late first century) reprise and heighten the celebration of birth. But in 1 Timothy 2, probably written only a generation or two later, birth is the only specified activity necessary for women to attain salvation, and it coordinates with a host of negatives: losing jewelry, nice clothes, and hairstyles; undertaking menial charities; shutting up; and giving up any work of the mind and any autonomous influence in the community.

Penitential Christian childbearing is women's primordial trump card damaged, the marring of their ordinary means to come out winners in the challenging game of fitting in and being happy as a wife in a patriarchal household. Not only were pagan wives rewarded with prestige and privileges once they had children, it also appears usual that when the head of the pagan household had as many children as he wanted, his wife was entitled to retire as a breeder. Husbands were on average much older than wives, and at any rate pagans had a sexual double standard; if a man had not yet lost interest in sex, he could go elsewhere. In other ways too, motherhood in traditional pagan society was not designed to be a burden. Among the Greeks and Romans, a typical matron was not oppressed by housework or childcare, as even modest households kept slaves to tend babies (or else hired nurses) and cook and clean. If her husband's treatment of her was intolerable—and in the community's eyes, that would have included inflicting a large number of offspring on her body and the family's energies and finances—a woman could declare a divorce and walk away. For the paterfamilias, a great drawback of owning the children was the sole material responsibility for them.

In contrast, a Christian mother of seven or eight children, whom the family couldn't afford, would have been in a woeful whipsaw. Her health was of course likely to be undermined by serial pregnancies. And as she was assigned menial work on moral and religious pretexts, from the start she labored more than a pagan wife of the same class. The growing family she was struggling to care for could hardly ingratiate her with a husband who needed to support that family. Add to this that he was not allowed to go elsewhere for sex and that the Christian church forbade divorce under most circumstances.[10]

Modern scholars tend to take at face value the attitude of the Pastoral Epistles' author and other early Christian authorities that churches had to maintain strict order and a reputation for propriety and harmlessness. Persecutors of Christians, after all, made them out to be everything from superstitious ignoramuses to incestuous perverts, cannibals, and insurrectionists. This was a compelling motivation for probity, but the trouble was that Christians acted increasingly like pagans without their redeeming practicality and humanism. Petty, purist tyrants could ride their communities hard.

Misogyny seems to be a signature vice of cultlike organizations. The hypnotic regularity with which cult or cultish leaders choose women as the ones who ought to suffer tends to keep the world at large from even noticing the choice, but this doesn't mean that the choice is inevitable or undeserving of scrutiny. Natural and common human reactions help explain one way that repellent, cultlike attitudes can develop even in an idealistic, happy community. In its fuller historical context, the targeting of Christian women strongly suggests a competitive backlash. Once there were spoils to divide (in this case, paid positions at the head of local Christian communities), women were kept out of activities for which they could expect recognition and rewards. In Judea during Jesus's lifetime, women had supported his mission financially, traveled with him, and welcomed him as a controversial guest in their homes. Several striking encounters with challenging women—a pushy, wise-cracking pagan; a Samaritan (that is, she belongs to a nation splintered long before from the Jews who worshipped in Jerusalem) who is living in sin; an adulterous woman caught in the act; and a prostitute who invades a dinner party to rub perfume on Jesus's feet—punctuate the stories of Jesus's travels and ministry. Women are able to change Jesus's mind about received ideas and make him flout the Jewish purity laws. They are permitted to touch and converse with him even if they are unrelated foreigners or sexual transgressors. The Gospels identify a total of seven women who stood by Jesus's cross, and only one man, John—and he does so in only one Gospel, the latest and the one named after him. Women alone went to Jesus's tomb to anoint his body, while his male followers cowered indoors.

Women were also among the early missionary Paul of Tarsus's bravest, most helpful, and most warmly praised followers; he commends a "deaconess," or female ritual servitor or general facilitator for the religious community, and permits women to preach, demanding only that they keep their veils on (probably a measure to prevent harassment).[11] During the persecutions, Christian women defied what professional torturers seem to have considered the special challenge of breaking them. You might think women would have been rewarded with leadership positions as the church took on more-solid institutional forms. You would be wrong.

Over time, their status in Christian society only diminished, and it is easy to see why. The author of the Pastoral Epistles sees them mainly as a threat to his own authority. He is preoccupied with the Christian household, and particularly with church leaders' homes as suspected fountainheads of ferment. These homes were to model tight obedience to the patriarch and flawless self-abnegation—on women's part most of all. Paul had hardly been concerned with the home; in his famous 1 Corinthians 7 passage, he recommends lifetime celibacy and lays down surprisingly open-minded and egalitarian rules for those who do choose to marry. In verse after verse, he favors participation in the new sect over the demands of a sexual partnership for both men and women. Paul mentions children only to assert that the offspring of pagan–Christian marriages are "pure" or "holy."[12]

The amendments written just two or three generations later are shattering. The author of the new Epistles decrees that once prospective Christian officials (all of them men) have passed an unspecified "test" and been appointed, their one specific, indispensable duty is to project their will downward onto women, children, and slaves, who will apparently have no appeal against them. The religious duties of all these other church members have no public expression; they fall under the heading of service and obedience to the patriarchs. For them, the unique new Christian elements of choice, conviction, and discernment—the working out of all individual salvation "with fear and trembling" that Paul speaks of in Philippians 2:12—have vanished.

Not even the household head is to enjoy the "freedom" Paul

praises while invoking the pagan ideal of political freedom of speech. Paul observes that a community cannot know a priori whether it is on the right spiritual path; instead, it needs to consider how well members behave and get on together—consideration that is of course impossible without open and fearless discussion.[13] But, again and again, the author of the Pastoral Epistles demands his readers avoid "wrangling over words." To this author, language other than his own is repeatedly denigrated as "empty" or "tainted/desecrated"; in 2 Timothy 2:17, it is said to spread "like gangrene."

The real Paul was an educated cosmopolitan and made use of many conventional rhetorical flourishes, the implication always being that his followers, let alone other people's, needed convincing. "Paul" of the Pastoral Epistles orders his readers not to listen to or associate with anyone who disagrees with him. Paul toggles between sternness and conciliation, with nuances of rancor, irony, glibness, tenderness, and caution. "Paul" has only one voice, that of self-righteousness and grievance, and only one interface with those who disagree: He reports how evil they are, sometimes attributing demonic influence and sometimes declaring them cursed or otherwise writing them off. In a faith leader, his use of the imagery of burning with red-hot irons is unnerving. He is a typical thin-skinned martinet, out of his depth, underqualified except in his aggression, sniffing out offenses and settling scores. Religion threatens to fall away as a mask near the end of 2 Timothy, where it sounds as if he is taking part in a petty feud. His words in 4:14–15 could have been scrawled on a wall or uttered by a drunken old man in a tavern: "Alexander the coppersmith behaved really terribly to me; the Master will pay him back for the things he did. You watch out for him too, because it was outrageous, the way he went against what we told him." (Again, this and other Bible translation, beyond single words and short phrases traditionally rendered, is my own.) That is the "royal we" of the tiny-minded tyrant's sulk, not the accepted leader's measured dignity.

Women come in as this author's chief preoccupation because women talk. It is their age-old reach toward public life. It is often their *only* pretension to public life, and they are (for all their educational deficits) quite good at it. Unless you cut their tongues out, they will go on voicing their views, in private if nowhere else. Homes therefore need tight control, and women especially tight control, because demonic voices of dissent enter through the home, discretely and under cover of hospitality.

For centuries before Jesus, both in Judea and in the Mediterranean region at large, folksy traveling pundits had claimed sustenance and shelter and propounded their views freely over dinner, with women listening even if they were mere servitors and then repeating what they had heard to other women. In their world, new ideas spread as if underground. An early Christian leader who didn't want competition had to try ruling in this sphere, as well as the sphere of casual male speech, because the elite pagan spheres of rhetorical higher education, the speaker's platform, and the law courts were closed to him. But casual, popular speech was maddeningly slippery; no qualifications applied. Cleverness might spring up anywhere; any nasty, sneaky, back-stabbing competitor could wiggle his way in—and women, the intellectual and moral subspecies, were the great betrayers. 2 Timothy 3 opens thus:

> 1 But know this: Daunting crises will manifest in the last days. 2 People will love only themselves and money, they will be boastful, arrogant, slanderous, disobedient to their par-

ents, ungrateful, unholy, 3 heartless, impossible to deal with, back-biters, without self-control, brutal, without regard for anything worthy, 4 treacherous, reckless, conceited, lovers of pleasure rather than lovers of God—5 having an appearance of reverence but denying its power. Have nothing to do with such people. 6 They are the kind who worm their way into homes and take captive the little womansies, who are loaded down with sins and led along by all kinds of passions, 7 always learning but never able to come to a knowledge of the truth.

The Greek diminutive for "woman" occurs only this once in the Bible, and here it spits with contempt. These are not human beings but donkeys, who are loaded down with poison, and they will take it in anywhere a sweet-talker leads them. The Pastoral Epistles' author seems to have an extremely broad definition of such deceptive communications, which in 1 Timothy 4:7 he calls "old women's tales." These might be anything not said or scripted by himself. No wonder that a little later, in 1 Timothy 5:14, the author wants women to do nothing but "marry, bear children, and manage their households, so as to give the opponent [Satan] no reason to revile us." That is, busy motherhood is the means par excellence of keeping women quiet.

A higher birthrate for Christians would have been enforceable in part through greater confinement. Women who sought family planning in the harsh and ignorant ancient medical environment needed a network, and the toil of caring in isolation for closely spaced babies could have easily sent mothers into a downward spiral of unwanted fertility. Another likely means of enforcing reproductive pliancy lay in the pious, sober, discrete older women whom the author of the Pastoral Epistles assigns to train young wives to "love their husbands, love their children, to be self-controlled, pure, busy at home, benevolent, and submissive to their husbands."[14] (I'm reminded of the Aunts in *The Handmaid's Tale*, who instruct, control, and spy on the fertile young Handmaids.) Yet another apparent means of control was to make past motherhood a qualification for the dole should a woman be widowed, as set out in 1 Timothy 5:10.

In sharp contrast to the many men who resisted Augustus's "pro-family" legislation, Christian husbands did not resist these new rules, as far as we can tell from contemporary and later evidence. The religion was mystical and paradoxical at its heart, and it was founded on startling propositions such as the world-governing divinity arising from the hinterland of the Judean province and being shamefully crucified. Christianity was thus wide open to pressure from an "overseer" or bishop with a fragile ego but stout ambitions. Such people grew their own branches of doctrine; the author of the Pastoral Epistles refers to branches other than his own, and "heresies" such as Gnosticism flourished. A well-established pagan cult had impressive temples, prestigious rituals, and the state as a benefactor. That *was* the religion, and it wasn't going to change. Christianity bubbled and frothed as a cauldron of competing intellectual systems. Any leader could throw in a sharp-tasting new ingredient by decreeing, for example, that married women should stay barefoot, pregnant, and in the kitchen, just because that was convenient for him.

But this particular ingredient had an intriguing flavor and stuck to the ribs and, in time, was universally accepted. This was, I believe, because Christianity increasingly partook of populist authoritarianism, which pits different disadvantaged groups against each other. Male Christians were on average not hugely more comfortable, secure, and powerful for being male. The majority of the sect's members labored under burdens such as enslavement, scanty or middling resources, and refugee status. Men who were able to start families were eager to hear about the importance of their position, and how to maintain it, and wives submitted even to bad terms for the sake of security and standing.

These couples were ripe for the teaching that their homes were, if lowly, morally superior if they were run according to God's plan as laid out in holy writ. Christians early on adopted the Jewish ban on infanticide, but did not adopt the idea that countless "seed" were an essential part of the survival and triumph that God promised his chosen people—an attitude that mandates respect for women as the fellow upholders of the household and nation.[15] Instead, the Christian teaching was grim: Women should be fertile as a punishment for being women. But when the hierarchy argued that fertility was a special debt of Christian women, distinguishing them from the godless mainstream society that Christians feared, resented, and condemned, the congregation was listening.

This was the start of a quiet but momentous change in the Roman and Roman-influenced world. No longer would social and material considerations necessarily govern family decisions, with older members (and especially the paterfamilias) drawing on experience and looking to indefinite future generations. Christians were encouraged to throw practicalities (limits of finance, health, time, space, and energy) to the wind, because God would eventually reward them. There could be lofty, sacrificial-sounding pretexts for what was basically an urge to put down and control women in an environment that had, in the past, proven ripe for developing public-facing roles for them.

Readers will of course think of similarities to conservative Christianity in poorer, more isolated parts of America, regions where women played significant roles in pioneering and in keeping struggling families and communities together during hardships (economic downturns, environmental disasters like the Dust Bowl), but where men have a fierce view of a zero-sum game for power and prestige. An even broader parallel to early Christianity's reproductive backlash dynamics is what happened to American women after World War II. During the war, they had poured into factories and shipyards and done well, and they would have been tough competition for returning servicemen. After the war, women were not only fired and banned from a range of industrial trades, but they were relegated to high rates of childbearing—a flood of propaganda argued that it was their nature and destiny—in isolating, labor-intensive suburbs, usually without servants or extended family to help them. In these places, important institutions—churches, hospitals, schools, businesses—were all new or reconstituted, and all reasoned in the interest of men.

Authoritarianism is normally as thin and friable—and as little nurturing—as a potato chip. Authoritarian movements don't typically last long, because their falsehoods and control tactics take too much energy to sustain over time, which was the case with McCarthyism, for example. But as certain successful authoritarians have found, imposed fertility is a wind-up-and-go mechanism. It comes into being as a paralyzing, silencing burden, and the burden is fairly easily multiplied. As I've noted, it takes assertiveness, ingenuity, and other resources to plan a family, especially for a woman in a community that is hostile to that; each wearing pregnancy will detract from the wherewithal to resist another.

The Pastoral Epistles are fascinating documents in that they lay out the basis for the loneliness, overwhelming responsibility, and self-loathing that in the Christian and Christian-shaped world made motherhood a legendary misery, and the relationships between mothers and children comparatively fraught. This is because Christian motherhood was designed not for the good of the mother, the family, or the clan, but to put women in their place and keep them there.

This is clear in these early texts. Pagans were of course no strangers to misogynist literature—the works of Semonides and Juvenal are most notable—but there misogyny ties up more closely to reality. After all, weren't women lazy, greedy, lecherous, and drunk, always up to no good at home while their husbands were out wrangling and toiling on behalf of the family? That wasn't an irrational set of suspicions and resentments in cultures in which wives customarily did not work in the fields but stayed indoors, making the minimal clothing necessary for mild or hot climates. Moreover, this literature grants exceptions to sweeping condemnations, and allows for male self-deprecation, humor, and even major concessions to logic.[16] Most importantly, there is no hostile general prescription, no basis for moving against women as a group, nothing with the lethal essence of what we class as hate speech, like "Round up all the immigrants!" or "Jews spread disease that threatens our nation." The pagan authors are just complaining, and they do not imagine that things can or ought to change.

The relentlessly illogical, mean-spirited, and punishing approach of the Pastoral Epistles when it comes to women is something new—though, sadly, not unfamiliar in modern America. The Pastoral Epistles take the typical paranoid, self-righteous behavior of arrivistes—especially their propensity to bully deserving people one tier down in the social hierarchy—and insist on giving it the status of religion and governance. Women are apt targets of this program. They are tough and adaptable; they make themselves useful—they have to. Their very presence is a challenge to men bent on perfecting the world through pointing and talking. And their fertility—which without men's goodwill they struggle to make the best use of—is an area of special vulnerability.

One telling feature of hate speech in the Pastoral Epistles is the particularly low quality of the discourse where women are concerned. Women are not flattered and argued with logically and learnedly, as in Paul's letters. In urging them in 1 Corinthians 11 to wear veils when they speak in the Christian assembly, for example, Paul speaks of the "glory" of their long hair, likely implying that their hair can be so beautiful, so enchanting, that it distracts men from what women are saying.

But now it is as if women are no longer in the audience to which such letters had been read aloud—and as if they are not even supposed to be concerned with the rationale by which their community is run: They are among the household slaves, children, and youths to whom patriarchs must deliver the rules. Women are banished from rhetoric, the public life of the mind to which the earlier Christian assemblies had admitted them, where they were allowed to "speak out" or "prophesy" whenever it moved them, just like the men, commenting on theology, their own feelings and lives, or the running of the assembly's affairs.

In the Pastoral Epistles, the sidelining of women seems to give free rein to a special dehumanization. While other subordinate groups are dealt with quite briefly and with relatively mild and familiar strictures (the slaves are not to pilfer or talk back, the youths are not to bother women), women are subjected to the kind of prolonged and self-contradictory bullying found in 1 Timothy 5. The passage concerns eligibility for the dole in the case of poor widows. Their plight is incontrovertible according to Jewish scripture, Jesus's teachings, and the experience of ascetic Jewish communities in Palestine, which Paul had supported as a fundraiser. One reason for helping widows was compelling both on humanitarian grounds and in the interest of a local group's integrity and reputation: A woman left without subsistence might sell her body in desperation. But the author of the Pastoral Epistles is having none of these facts or this logic:

> 3 Give stipends to the widows who are really widows. 4 But if a widow has children or grandchildren, they must first learn to show reverence toward their own family and make recompense to their forebearers, for this is acceptable in the sight of God. 5 The true widow, who is left all alone, puts her hope in God and persists night and day in her pleas and prayers. 6 But the one who cavorts around is dead even while she is still alive. 7 Give these orders, so that people will be above reproach. 8 If anyone does not provide for his own people, and especially his own household, he has negated his religious belief and is worse than an unbeliever.

When it came to widows in the ancient world, there couldn't in reality have been much doubt about whose husband was dead and who was destitute. The lashing out at families unwilling to take on their traditional or merely imputed responsibilities reminds me of American political conservatives' favorite rationale for why no guaranteed social safety net is needed: What about the family?

The trouble, of course, was that a person in dire need, and the church authorities as well, would have been hard put to *force* a family to help out, if in fact it could. Typical American attempts at long-term enforcement for alimony and child-support payments are a sobering illustration. Roman law, though it was even less efficient, did require children to support their needy parents. Also, city administrations and rich men handed out doles. But, alas, the Christian church forbade its members from resorting to the pagan government's courts with their disputes, and the church had its own exclusive system of doles. Moral, social, and commercial claims of all sorts were supposed to be settled within the Christian community, away from heathens' contagious wickedness. But, alas again, that community could enforce practically nothing, only exclude members who didn't comply with what it enjoined; and leaders were naturally slow to move against better resourced and more influential members, who of course included themselves. Such neglect of internal accountability was particularly easy when the wronged were isolated, needy, and female.

The author of the Pastoral Epistles knows that he can say anything, and that women cannot hold him to account. Therefore, when faced with inconvenient facts and religious traditions, the author redefines the word for "widow" to mean a widow with a thoroughly vetted claim to the church's support—and the rest of the passage makes clear that no one would qualify. For every established, urgent obligation of the church, there will be a dodge.

The washing of hands in the passage above culminates in the command to widows who are left alone to pray fervently and unceasingly. Given that some will be on the street with their young children without the Church's help, these verses have all the moral cogency of responding to a school shooting with thoughts and prayers, except that here the author does not even claim to be praying himself.

Glancing toward the alternative, a widow who takes no toll on the Christian community because her invested dowry returns to her, or because some other resource provides a dignified livelihood, the author bridles in added disgust: Her independence must mean that she is "cavorting"—a living death in his eyes. He is drawing on common imagery that equates an overfed, frisky farm animal with a thoughtless, sensual human being. The idea here is that a woman becomes subhuman when means are at her own disposal.

What about the perfect candidate for assistance whom we are about to hear described, the elderly widow who has always lived simply, cared for her dependents, and supported the church with her unpaid labor? For this author, dealing fairly with this sublime exception would mean squaring his rigid circle, which is the persecution of widows for being widowed. He squirms like a netted alligator as he tries to divest the church from any obligations to assist in emergencies with the heavy burdens it has all but forced women to take on: the children they have borne for the sake of salvation (not for the well-being of themselves and their family), as well as the habit of servile, unpaid, isolated labor that would have made it hard to suddenly maneuver toward making a livelihood.

> 9 A widow should be enrolled if she is at least sixty years old, has been married only once, 10 and is well known for good deeds such as bringing up children, entertaining strangers, washing the holy ones' feet, imparting relief to the afflicted, and devoting herself to every good work. 11 But refuse to enroll younger widows. For when their passions draw them

away from Christ, they want to marry, 12 and thus they come in for condemnation because they are setting aside their initial commitment. 13 At the same time, they also learn to be lazy, gadding around from house to house; and they are not only lazy, but also gossips and busybodies, speaking of things they shouldn't. 14 So I wish the younger widows to marry, have children, and manage their households, denying the adversary any opportunity for abusive language. 15 For some have already turned aside to follow Satan. 16 If any believing woman has widows in her family, she must help them and not allow the church to be burdened, so that it can help those who are truly widows.

To set such a high age qualification for the dole was effectively to withhold it. Sixty was an advanced age in antiquity, and most women who survived to it had been widowed years earlier, as husbands tended to be considerably older. How was a poor widow—who was not supposed to marry a second time—to survive, bringing up her children and engaging in expensive and time-consuming charities, without slaves doing the hardest and dirtiest work in her home? This is the concrete meaning of "washing the holy ones' feet"—foot-washing was normally a slave's job, and in the Gospels, it is an extraordinary show of self-abnegation. But the Christian wife and mother is to do it for any "holy ones" who show up at her door for food and lodging, and must attend to any other needs in the community. What will be left of her by the time she is eligible to apply for assistance as a widow?

The history of the Christian movement to this point leaves her further exposed. A woman who was sixty in 120 CE, a plausible date for the writing of the Pastoral Epistles, was born in the year

60, when Jesus's followers comprised a few tiny squiggles on the religious map. The chance that she was raised in the sect is infinitesimal, to say nothing of the chance that she was raised with the kind of values expressed in the Pastoral Epistles. During the era of Paul and likely for some time afterward, women were still testing the limits of outspokenness and involvement. A woman who grew up Christian back then would be more liable for punishment than reward in her old age, because of what she had grown used to getting away with in her youth.

Verses 11 through 13—denigrating both women's desire to marry again and their inevitable careless and self-damning behavior when single—look close to nonsensical. If the goal was to keep women off the dole and under household control, then it would have been best to have them remarry, as the author concedes immediately after this, in Verse 14. Therefore, any expectation that they not remarry serves only as a stick to beat them with. Whatever women do, they can't do it in the right way, measuring up to the miraculous widow who wishes neither to marry nor to remain single, and who somehow manages to keep up her costly charitable giving and services without any assured income, and thus no morally ruinous financial independence.

The author's crowning inspiration comes in Verse 16: He pushes the problem of supporting widows onto other women, although there is no sign that he would authorize these women to set aside the money they would need for such a commitment-heavy undertaking later on. Verses 9 and 10 seem to indicate that women are *always* supposed to tap themselves out to their full extent, so where would their surplus to support each other come from? In any event, I'm reminded of Newt Gingrich pushing the problem of inadequate public education resources for children of the poor onto children of the poor: They can save the taxpayers' money by working for free as janitors in schools, and this will inculcate the values they sorely need. Anything is held to be less outrageous than that those with money, and with the established obligation to part with it for the benefit of the needy, actually do so.

On top of all this, in Verses 17 and 18, the author immediately rubs women's noses in their disadvantages. "Elders who lead effectively are to be held worthy of double payment, especially those who work hard at preaching and teaching. For the Scripture says, 'Do not muzzle an ox while it is treading out the grain,' and, 'The worker deserves to be paid.'"[17] Thus women are to work without limits and without pay and have almost no hope of humanitarian relief in their most common crisis, widowhood, while the male hierarchy ("elders" probably covers bishops or "overseers," deacons, other ministerial assistants, and any other men who regularly act in the church's name) was to have a 100 percent raise to reward them if, basically, they were unstinting in exacting work and conformity from others. According to his words here and his own example in composing the Pastoral Epistles, this is what the author thinks worthy leadership consisted of. He is therefore authorizing the doubling of his own salary.

Underlying all statements about women in these Epistles is a new, uncompromising kind of hatred. From this period on, Christian wives struggled to regain what pagan and Jewish wives had never lost: the status of human beings and the credit for being stakeholders with dignity in their own sphere.

It would take several further books for me just to outline the consequences of this attitude in subsequent history; but I can at least foreshadow them, offering a prelude in miniature. In my mind, the first few centuries of Christianity, before the so-called

Dark Ages (starting with the fifth century and ending around the tenth), are bookended by two families. In the first Christian century, there is the mother Mary of Nazareth, probably a widow, in a rural backwater, with her seven children, among them the itinerant preacher Jesus, whom the Romans crucified. In the fourth century, there were Patricius and Monica in North Africa, with their family of a large but unknown size—but too big: They could afford to fully educate only one of their sons, Augustine. Mary's family lived amid tumult and suffering: banditry, mass poverty and underemployment, insurrection, violent religious conflict—troubles that would culminate in a great military clash and Rome's genocidal victory when Jerusalem fell in 70 CE. Augustine was also born into a world of fierce conflict over diminishing resources. He wrote *The City of God* in part to comfort Rome for its sacking by the Visigoths in 410, and he died in 430, cooped up during the siege of the metropolis Hippo Regius (in what is now Algeria) by the Vandals.

Such disasters presaged the age when a population center's main purpose wasn't the pursuit of an array of duties, comforts, enjoyments, and ambitions, but to provide safety behind crude walls from attack and plunder. I believe that none of the chaos in early-modern Europe would have been as bad if women had kept the status they enjoyed in Greco-Roman antiquity—and particularly if they and their husbands had had only as many children as they themselves wanted.

CHAPTER 3

IT'S THE BABY, STUPID

Augustine's Neurosis, Our Theocracy

CHRISTIAN TEACHINGS ABOUT CELIBACY HAD MEAsured and moderate-sounding origins. About twenty years after Jesus's mission, the earliest New Testament writer, Paul of Tarsus, wrote in the First Letter to the Corinthians that for those gifted with sexual self-restraint, it was better to stay unmarried: This would allow both men and women happy lives of undistracted religious devotion.[1] But among the Church Fathers of later antiquity were some who promoted celibacy as a ferocious cult, a means of fleeing women's polluting company and consorting only with ethereal fellow men, who were the true image of God. Origen, a theologian active during the first half of the third century, is said to have castrated himself when he could not repress his carnal desires.

It was Augustine the bishop of Hippo (354–430), the greatest of the Church Fathers, who set the seal on an extreme ideology and culture of celibacy. He was born to a Christian mother and a pagan father in a small town in Romanized North Africa and trained in oratory, the most essential skill for public life. He was so talented that, though he lacked family money and connections, he eventually won an elite teaching post in Milan, then the Roman imperial capital.

It was there that several great stresses in his life converged. First, there was the question of his religious commitment. He had joined the heretical Manichaean branch of Christianity while still a student, but he rather quickly became skeptical and unhappy there. Metaphysical conundrums continued to torment him long after he was drawn to the state-sponsored Catholic (or "universal") branch of Christianity that was to bequeath its basic ideas and practices to later ages.

Augustine's Christian mother had long applied embarrassing, harassing moral pressure, particularly over sexual purity. But he had a long-term mistress—possibly with his mother's cooperation or complaisance, because the relationship gave a stable outlet to his libido—to whom he was deeply attached and who gave him a son. In Milan, he had to turn his back on the mistress when he became engaged to a young girl from a wealthy family—apparently a match his mother took the lead in brokering—and all the while he was spiritually and intellectually drawn to celibacy. On top of all this, he agonized over the question of his vocation. He found teaching exhausting, frustrating, and trivial, and reciting panegyrics to the emperor (a required sideline) humiliating; he longed to retire to a contemplative life. This didn't mean, however, that he had lost his hunger for audiences; he just wanted his own meditations to guide the terms in which he addressed them—a tough ambition for a parvenu, overworked teacher, and courtier.

Augustine began to resolve these conflicts through his "conversion" in the year 386. This was not his mere submission to established Christian doctrine; rather, he recovered from an emotional breakdown with the help of revelations peculiar to himself, which moved him to be baptized and embark on a life of celibacy and pious study rather than marriage. About two years later, after his mother's death, he returned to North Africa and set up his own small religious community with his intimates. In time, he was recruited as a priest and later promoted to bishop.

Under church auspices, Augustine became an extremely important preacher, controversialist, and developer of Christian doctrine. He wrote two classics of religious literature, *Confessions* and *The City of God*, as well as a huge array of other works. He had more to say than any other single person about what Catholicism would look like and, because Catholicism reigned almost exclusively in Western Europe for around a thousand years, more than any other single person about what Christianity would look like.

Augustine was a hardline advocate of celibacy. When he founded the first Catholic religious order—that is, the first monastic community under church sponsorship—it was strictly for men who renounced sex and marriage. To give some context, this was an era in which celibacy was not yet a hard and fast rule, even for Catholic clerics; an important bishop who was Augustine's contemporary, Synesius, had a wife and children and a family estate.

In opposing marriage, Augustine was not a misogynist at

the level of certain other Church Fathers. He was not a venomous name-caller or a creepy haranguer and controller of women, though he did endorse teachings on women's lower nature and the dangers they posed to men's spiritual elevation. He actually wrote a treatise, *On the Good of Marriage*, which emphasized companionship, fidelity, and procreation as social goods.

But Augustine's thinking on women, sex, and (above all) fertility tended toward the absolutist; it went further than the outright misogynist Church Fathers' thinking in its surrealistic rigidity, cold exclusionism, and emphasis on enforcement. I believe this is because his opinions on this topic were not mainly theological or theoretical or cultural in origin, and not a matter of sectarian prescription or popular prejudice or anything else he might have been able to put at some distance from himself and not pursue to its logical (or illogical) extreme with a passion and determination that, in him, appear unique. His thinking on celibacy was instead deeply personal, a matter of experience from early boyhood. His own closest relationships were never anything but hideously complicated, and his longing to be free of the resulting anxiety, guilt, and shame was poison for his doctrinal legacy.

He does not hide his painful ambivalence about his mother. Memorializing her in his *Confessions*, he performs joint-popping rhetorical gymnastics to formally defend traits that the reader has no trouble naming in plain words: superstition, sanctimony, wild clinginess, manipulation, and greed and ambition that used a troubled child as their instrument.

Augustine carried heavy guilt from a brief youthful wild-oats period—though it was likely only his mother's influence that made what was in this era an ordinary male rite of passage seem wicked to him. But the guilt about promiscuity, significantly, didn't compare to the guilt he felt about his one long and committed erotic relationship. For years he couldn't bear the thought of living without the mistress whom strict Christian morality forbade him; he remained "faithful to her bed," and he felt mutilated by grief after she was sent away to facilitate his betrothal. He adored the child they had together while at the same time he suffered from excoriating shame over the child's illegitimate birth.

We tend to pay the most attention to the element of romantic tragedy in Augustine's personal life, but that is what we have been brought up to focus on. Augustine probably couldn't have imagined Hollywood, the Hallmark Channel, or anything else that touts the imperative need for a life-defining soul-mate. Neither pagan nor early Christian males placed a relationship with a woman, even a beloved wife, anywhere near as high as modern Western males place it; in fact, emotional dependence on a woman was not supposed to be an assurance of transcendent meaning but rather a sign of weakness and distraction. Augustine was a man of his time and his culture; he loathed himself for allowing a woman to keep him back from changes in his life he felt were essential.

Accordingly, she is a bit player in his story of triumph and liberation in the *Confessions*. Her lover of more than a decade does not name her or touch on her personality or her background or appearance; a very short passage records their separation and her departure for Africa alone. But his attitude toward their son Adeodatus ("Given by God") is enormously different, reflecting the normal hierarchy of relationships among the ancient Romans: A male child was the center of the universe and the main reason to have a female partner in the first place.

Augustine was devoted to Adeodatus; he does not hold back

praise from the boy, though he was illegitimate. It is clear in the first book of the *Confessions* that Augustine watched over the infant as he grew self-aware, asserted his will, and learned to communicate. This author has been called the founder of child psychology. His analysis is marred by his insistence on judging even a baby sinful for crying and wanting his way; but otherwise he is insightful in his remarks.

Augustine educated his growing child meticulously and enthusiastically, had him baptized along with himself, and later made him the star of his dialogue *The Teacher*. In this, Augustine somewhat resembles the famous Roman orator Quintilian, who evidently believed that it was impossible to train a young orator too thoroughly and who memorialized two extremely promising sons who died as little boys in the preface to *Training in Oratory*. But *The Teacher* is supposed to have been based on a conversation with Adeodatus when the boy was a teenager, and—whether this is mostly true, or mostly fond fiction—shows a discerning, appealing, and forthright young mind, a perfect illustration of the argument that, though the right teacher can help to evoke worthy insight, knowledge is preexisting.

Adeodatus's death, which may have occurred during the same year that Augustine wrote *The Teacher*, must have been a wound far worse than the loss of a mistress who, attractive and accommodating as she might have been and strong as their erotic bond evidently was, would not have stimulated his mind, reflected well on him in public, or inspired high-minded hopes in him for the future. And losing Adeodatus must have brought a whole hornet swarm of regrets to needle the wound of loss.

Augustine was excited and deeply satisfied to give up both his teaching career and his hopes of a high-flying political one, which might have been attainable through the wealthy marriage his mother had helped broker for him. He withdrew for contemplation, study, and intellectual communion, first in Italy and then back in Africa, with a group that included Adeodatus, whose talents he could now cultivate at leisure. He was convinced that God had placed him on the right road and would bless his endeavors, not least his endeavors as a father. Even though he had become a father through sin, God was letting him make it right and turn it to a lofty purpose. The son named as God's gift would be a glorious testimony to God's grace. These reassuring thoughts crashed into a stone wall in the form of Adeodatus's death, after which Augustine was apparently so demoralized that he took a break from his religious enclave.

In Augustine's guilty, self-loathing grief, I see an extra excruciation due to the marriage he had let his mother arrange for him. We do not know the background of his young fiancée's family, but we know that the frustrated and put-upon teacher dreamed that such a marriage might allow him to become a provincial governor—a step or two below the emperor. From the start, however, he would have had to play a high-stakes game of service and ingratiation in high circles.

There was not the slightest chance that his in-laws would have let him keep his illegitimate son close, or continue cultivating the boy's gifts. The young wife was to have legitimate children, with whom Adeodatus would not have been allowed to compete. He might have gone into some sort of menial exile or met with an unfortunate accident or ailment (such as was common in the imperial household, with which this family might have been associated). From the start, the prospective in-laws must have viewed with distress the long-established but jury-rigged household in which Adeodatus was growing up; in fact, they helped break it up by requiring, or just accepting, the banishment of his mother, Augustine's mistress, to another continent.

Augustine had to have realized the trap he had fallen into by agreeing to marry into a powerful family, which would mean bringing with him a vulnerable stepson, perhaps without even the status of a Roman citizen, as his mother may have been a slave. The emotional agony Augustine suffered during the period right before his embrace of mainstream Christianity and his choice of a celibate life had several causes, including damage to his health from years of speaking in a raised voice; by this time, he apparently *couldn't* teach, or orate in public either, so he would have feared that his many years of training and experience were wasted. He does not mention anxiety over his son's future, which would have been uppermost in the mind of any loving Roman father, and Augustine certainly was one. I believe that this is because his willingness to virtually abandon his son to get ahead himself was a matter too shameful, too painful to write of, even for this unusually frank author. A Roman might as well cut off his own arm or leg as betray his son. But this is exactly what Augustine had done.

Adeodatus was an only child, so when he died, Augustine was completely bereft of offspring. The likely cause of the boy's lack of siblings would have worsened the father's guilt. Contrary to the church's firm disapproval (though there was no outright or enforced ban yet), which Augustine was to second in his doctrinal writings, he and his mistress probably used contraception or had recourse to abortions. As the great scholar of late antiquity Robin Lane Fox points out, the couple remained lovers for thirteen years after the birth of their child and so must have compounded the sin of their relationship itself "in widely practiced ways."[2]

No wonder, then, that Augustine fantasized for the rest of his life about a world without the risks and responsibilities that sex can bring with it. He records in the *Confessions* a vision he had just before his conversion. Two allegorical characters representing delay and foolishness hold him back, but Chastity or Self-Restraint "in her pure decorum" intervenes and rivets Augustine's attention.

> She was calm, and not lax in her lightheartedness. She honorably sweet-talked me, telling me to come and not delay, and she extended reverent arms to lift me up and embrace me. She already held whole flocks of people who could teach me by example: no end of boys and girls were there, and many people in early adulthood—but every age was represented, including serious-minded widows and elderly virgins, and among all these people, Self-Restraint was anything but barren: she was a fruitful mother whose sons were joys begotten from you, Master, her lawful husband. . . .
>
> I blushed like fire, because I was still hearing the muttering of my frivolities; I kept delaying and was up in the air. Again Self-Restraint seemed to speak: "Deafen yourself to those dirty parts of your body that live on this earth, so that they're killed off. They tell you stories of delights, but the law of the Master your God has more about delights to tell you."[3]

Self-Restraint is a paradoxical seductress. She urges Augustine to embrace her by turning away from the influence of desire.

She is irresistible as few lecturers and preachers are, the kind of woman who can make a man do anything she likes at the mere sight of her and the sound of her voice. She represents artful and manipulative persuasion. She "sweet-talks" him—the established language for a prostitute—but honorably. Her "charm" (the English translation I would now choose instead of "decorum") is "pure." She is without desire herself and seeks only his joy and immortality. She is not a huckster of words and images but a tender and loving nurturer of innumerable offspring. In her copious motherhood, she recalls an Eastern fertility goddess, the Great Mother, with her many tiers of bare breasts, but Self-Restraint has acquired her children without sex, and in fact through her condemnation of sex. As recruits for chastity (rather than for Christianity per se), her progeny are all beyond childhood, but they are perfectly cared for, passive, and happy in Self-Restraint's arms, because she is the perfect mother, relieving them of all that they are not equipped to hazard and endure.

This is one man's strange vision in the extremes of his individual stress. And according to the *Confessions*, the vision only dredged up Augustine's misery from its depths and sent him running from his friend Alypius to throw himself sprawling on the ground in uncontrollable weeping for a resolve that he could not muster.

Clearly, Augustine's vision did not help him move toward any resolution of the whipsaws from which he was suffering. He was an aspiring Christian flayed with guilt over relationships to which he felt physically, emotionally, and—as a provider and a faithful lover—morally bound. He was a paterfamilias who could not secure his dependents' future, and he was a born intellectual who, without leisure, could not pursue the big questions that tantalized him. Augustine's allegory of Self-Restraint is a rescue fantasy, promising that limitations like his own could magically melt away, but it was a false promise. I believe he fled and sobbed uncontrollably because he viscerally knew he couldn't have it all and was tantalized beyond endurance.

A little later, in the same garden, he came across Bible verses that he represents as instantly resolving his inner conflict, so that he decided on the spot to be baptized and undertake a celibate, contemplative life. The verses urge withdrawal from raucous partying, drunkenness, promiscuity, and feuding rivalry, and a replacement of the body's desires with devotion to Jesus (Romans 13:13–14). Augustine was not in fact indulging his body's desires with riotous living; he may have merely seized on the ideas of withdrawal and physical desire. Perhaps the overall irrelevance of the verses was helpful to him by providing a convenient dodge in a psychological emergency. He had just had a hysterical, trapped reaction to an actual confrontation, through the vision of Self-Restraint, with his most fundamental choice: sex and family or celibacy. By relying on these verses as an alternative revelation, he could calmly renounce the rollicking and boisterous sins he didn't indulge in and have the appearance of making an important resolve.

Augustine's vision of Self-Restraint, so obviously sprung from the unresolvable dilemmas of his personality and situation, is thus an unaddressed wrinkle in the narrative. The powerful revelation comes to him, but it is quite quickly put aside without being interpreted, let alone integrated into his life. Nor did the vision take on any active, inspirational role that I know of in ongoing Christian thought. It would have had tough competition in the veneration of the Virgin Mary. Through the Virgin, the Spirit becomes flesh by means of another fleshly being's unfailing acceptance, love, and care, which raise her to the status of a heavenly being. Without her, the world cannot be saved; through her, human motherhood becomes holy. In dismal contrast, Self-Restraint stands only for a mash-up of impossibilities as hallucinated by one man at the end of his rope.

Have an impossible dream of perfect happiness as a sexual being and an asexual one at the same time, then run for celibate retirement as the nearest exit from the agony of the human condition: This is the essence of Augustine's storied conversion. The exit was a narrow one, however, and to get through it, he would have to slice off large parts of himself—and not only himself. He ended up not only radically distorting his own humanity, but weaving distortions into Christian culture so tightly that they could never be completely extricated.

On the doctrinal level, he eventually went after an essential role of women that earlier Church Fathers had not managed to denigrate completely: procreative marital sex, activated by male desire and effective through the pleasurable male orgasm—all a part of God's plan for creation, right? To those guided by the Bible, God in Genesis 1:28 gives the command to be fruitful and multiply. For the early Christians, sex might have been sanctioned only in marriage, and marriage might have been deemed the choice of the weak and low-minded, but for their leaders to place fertile marriage beyond the pale of fully submissive obedience to God would have been neither scriptural nor practical.

But this was before Augustine amended the Genesis story in order to associate sexual desire, in itself, with the fall of disobedient humankind into sin, misery, and death. In *The City of God*, the greatest work of his old age, Augustine wrote of desire-free intercourse in unspoiled, innocent Eden, intercourse that was *truly* obedient to God and without a trace of human will or willfulness.

To Augustine, heterosexual sex as we know it, with its indispensable fuel of male desire, was a token of humanity's first, and most fatal, rebellion. It should be possible, and it *was*, he argues at length, to have sex without "lust," calmly, dutifully, for the divinely decreed purpose of begetting children, and for nothing else. That was how it was before the temptation, the fall from grace, and Adam and Eve's expulsion from an earthly paradise.[4]

This interpretation of Genesis was not of a piece with Augustine's general puritanism. True, he harbored compunctions about pleasure, satisfaction, curiosity, and aspiration in general. But concerning other areas of enjoyment and self-assertion than sex, his harshest statements tend to be counter-balanced by expressions of open-mindedness and even whimsy, and by his overarching principle that God had created nothing evil; therefore natural joys, as part of God's creation, should remain joyful and the basis of thankfulness and praise. Outside of intercourse, Augustine is broadly uncertain where lines between reverent purposes and sensory and emotional experiences should be drawn. How effective, for example, was a particular kind of music in drawing the mind to God through beauty? He even excuses—more like shrugs off—the sexual dreams and nocturnal emissions he continued to experience: "The gap itself between the two kinds of occurrences [i.e., waking and sleeping ejaculations] reveals to us that it wasn't we ourselves who did what, in any event, we're sorry happened within us—however it happened."[5] As a young man, Augustine had gay encounters. He later denounced these as friendship polluted, but he did not become a persecutory homophobe; the acts, though definitely sins in this thinking, played only a walk-on role in the drama of his life and ideology.

It was only heterosexual coupling—even in marriage blessed by the Bible and the church—that haunted his mind as fundamentally wrong, and by the time he wrote *The City of God* Augustine was convinced that sex was something not created to be as people actually experience it. It sounds instead like a sort of super-advanced robotic agriculture, with the man channeling the pure will of his maker and the woman reduced to the role of inert seedbed, not only without desire or pleasure but even without a sense of human relationships that are important in their own right: partner, lover, mother. Considering the negotiations, festivity, commitments, ornamentation, and prestige around a young woman's legitimate deflowering in ancient cultures, and women's considerable dignity as wives and mothers, even the *idealized*, prelapsarian Christian Eve of Augustine is demoted by a universe.

The imagery of the best imaginable wife as not even an agent in her most essential, most esteemed function of reproduction may go some way toward explaining the widespread silencing, immobilizing, and blanking out of the gender in the centuries when Augustine's doctrines, more than any others, shaped Catholicism and Catholicism shaped European societies. Women lost or saw diminished their rights to inherit, own, and manage property; to sign contracts; to go to court to redress wrongs against themselves; and even rights pertaining to their survival, such as the right to withdraw from or resist husbands working their way up to murder. The Augustinian ideal of the woman who lies perfectly still, who does not have a thought, feeling, or voice about what is happening to her because she is not even the channel through which the holy will to procreate descends—her husband is—was reified in custom and law.

AUGUSTINE ALSO INFLICTED HIS DEEP ANXIETIES AND suspicions about heterosexual desire institutionally as the founder of Catholic monasticism. There had long been monks; Anthony of Egypt was a background inspiration for Augustine's own conversion. But "monk" comes from the Greek word meaning "solitary," a hermit who lived in the wilderness, because in a city it was impossible to be left alone in prayer, and early monastic communities developed as independent bodies in isolated places, without coordination or supervision by the church hierarchy. Augustine brought monasticism within the church, and he wrote the first monastic rule, for the order to be known as the Augustinians. With his new power to shape the lives of younger men, he showed himself preoccupied with deterring them from what he considered the greatest source of spiritual and moral difficulty: erotic desire for women as sexual and domestic partners.

Augustine did write letters to female religious, and there is even a version of the rule for convents, but his great concern was for men and their purity. For a celibate family of brothers, the symbolic father was supposed to have no aim more ferocious than to head off the drive that is the basis of biological families. Given the robust post-adolescent age at which men tended to undertake Christian celibacy,[6] the policing must have been no small task. Augustine took up the rhetorical side of the job with zest and concentration. Here is part of the passage in *The*

Rule of Saint Augustine (as it is known now) that he devotes to this topic:

> Whenever you go out, walk together; when you get to where you are going, stay together.... Although your eyes may happen to fall on some woman, they must be fixed on no one.... When you go out, you are not banned from seeing women, but it is an offense to pursue them or to want them to pursue you. It is not only by touch or emotion but also by looking that lust for women pursues and is pursued. And you must not say that you have pure minds if you have impure eyes, because an impure eye is the announcer of an impure heart. And even if the tongue is silent, when impure hearts announce themselves to each other through a gaze that goes back and forth, and there is a delightful mutual heat from the body's lust, chastity in its essence flees from behavior at a run, though the bodies are as yet untouched and there is no sullying violation of them.
>
> Whoever fixes his eyes upon a woman and loves to have hers fixed on him should not think that others do not see what he is doing. He is absolutely seen, even by those he thinks do not see him....
>
> And do not accuse yourself of viciousness if you bring this offense to light. In fact, you are to blame if you let your brothers be ruined through your silence, when you can correct them by turning them in....
>
> Once [a brother suspected of interest in a woman] is convicted ... he must be punished in a way that will reform him.... If he refuses to submit to the punishment, he must be expelled from your community if he does not leave willingly. This is not an act of cruelty, but of compassion, so that

he does not destroy many others through polluting, disease-bearing contact with him. . . .

But if anyone should go so grievously wrong as to receive a letter or small gifts of any sort clandestinely from any woman, you ought to take pity on him and pray for him if he confesses this of his own accord. But if he is caught in the act and found guilty, he must be more severely corrected according to the judgment of the priest or the head of the community.[7]

Life in a religious community is complicated, as Augustine would have been the first to admit. There are going to be quarrels, sulking, malingering, and all kinds of other efforts to shirk the unfamiliar burdens and restrictions. The head of a community, who can command obedience, might have a bad attitude himself. But while acknowledging all of this and more throughout other parts of the Rule, Augustine tends to be confident about the power of brotherly love, self-control, tolerance, forgiveness, and special institutional structures to engender discipline. He directs, for example, that clothing come from a common storeroom and be sent back to a common laundry. This will remove any opportunity for a man to lay claim to preferred items.

Outside the part of the Rule concerning the lure of impure thoughts, Augustine very seldom, and without any apparent neurotic jitters, resorts to severely judgmental words. Most strikingly to me, he argues that brooding hatred is tantamount to murder, and he declares that a man who will not ask for forgiveness does not belong in a monastery.[8] But these harsh judgments are fleeting, mitigated by much gentler context, and without mandates for punishments attached. In fact, it is stated that the man who resists reconciliation might not be dismissed from the monastery.

But the section of Augustine's rules for monastic life that concerns purity of thought is a frenzy of projections. Full of detailed, repetitive, abundantly rationalized fear-mongering—above I have reproduced only the most salient passages, to minimize tedium—it is the longest segment in the Rule text, and gives a strikingly persecutory impression. Alleging that monastic brothers are harrowingly prone to pollute the community with their sexual gazes, Augustine insists on the need for surveillance, reporting, an inquisitorial process, and severe punishment.

The laser focus on sexual temptation by strange women, and in public, seems acutely personal, and linked to women's reproductive capacity. What arguably makes searing to him the thought of locking eyes with an attractive woman in public is his own history of doing it, and finding over time that the consequences were momentous and lastingly tragic. He writes in the *Confessions* of picking up a woman during a church service.[9] The chronology actually works for this to be his mistress and the mother of his son.

Now, apparently, he believes that if not for the danger of locking eyes with a woman, monks could safely walk alone outside their private sanctuary. No other peril or temptation in public spaces except the presence of women is cited in the entire Rule. The repression of sexual urges requires a diligence and minuteness in surveillance that is typical of a totalitarian state. A voice suitable for a modern tyrant or cult leader even asserts that thoughts are *not* free: Privacy within the individual mind is an illusion, and people should live in dread that their failures to surrender their deepest selves to the community's demands are written all over them. In fact, so terrible is the danger of pernicious thoughts and feelings originating from the sight of a woman's face that no one must feel guilty about what is (plainly and rationally) a betrayal: turning in a companion for his thoughts alone, and—worse still—for natural and ordinary thoughts such as the betrayer is very likely to have too.

The dire danger of the sight of a woman *in itself*, so that the community may need to pile on preemptively to prevent sexual misconduct and ruin, is a topic without any tradition in scripture. From the Hebrew Bible through the Apocrypha through the New Testament, men are tempted, and they resist or they don't. They are always free to choose, and the onus is on them as individuals, not on a community that needs to control them.[10]

It was the Church Fathers, but especially Augustine, who pushed the idea of erotic anthrax imbibed through the eye. The bishop of Hippo's rarified, relentless hatred of the sex drive must have come from his particular, and particularly painful, experience as a young man. Many men, Christians included, had mistresses. But to acknowledge, bring up, and cherish an illegitimate child was not at all common. Augustine was bold and committed in doing it, and punished in proportion by his conscience for the way things turned out.

In this light, it makes sense that, while insisting on God's love, Augustine clung to images of God's unrelenting punishment for giving in to the most natural lures of conscious attention: above all, the look between a man and a woman that eventually leads to the birth of a child in an unfriendly world. During the siege of Hippo by the Vandals, during his mortal illness, Augustine kept reading penitential Psalms that he had ordered to be copied and hung on the wall near hear him, and he wept steadily and abundantly. The ecstatic devotion he had felt while reciting the Psalms in the weeks after his conversion, his embrace of God as the perfect, all-giving lover, had yielded to an obsession with God as the pure punisher, who would not, until the last instant of life (if then), tolerate his slave being human, having his own irreducible needs and impulses toward joy. The brightest hope—too late for Augustine—was to try to turn young men into pious robots so that late in their lives they would have no past like his to agonize over.

IT WOULD HARDLY BE FAIR TO BLAME ONE INTELLECTUAL, no matter how eminent, for the character of the age that came after him, but certainly Augustine's thinking about sex and marriage added to the backwardness and miseries of the so-called Dark Ages, to which I was looking ahead at the end of chapter 2 as well. Granted, many things made that period dark: barbarian invasions, the loss of Roman institutions and infrastructure, and Christian innovations that had nothing to do with the family, one example being the commerce-stunting ban the church placed on the charging of interest.

But Augustine, with his preoccupying fretting about reproductive sex, was immensely influential. Alfred the Great (the ninth-century Anglo-Saxon king who stopped the advance of the Vikings and laid the foundations of English civilization) read him; far-flung monasteries enforced his rules. I've already remarked that his ideas were likely a factor in women's massive loss of rights during the Middle Ages. More certainly, these ideas hindered the formation of families and reduced their status and power, and this inflicted general and systematic harm on the functioning of European societies.

Families tend to be interconnected, outward- and forward-looking, and dynamic. They are the most productive and sustaining part of human culture in many ways beyond the biological. Now, for the first time in the history of the West, much of the wealth, power, prestige, security, knowledge, and skills that had belonged to families migrated out of them and fell into the hands of those who joined the priesthood and celibate religious communities. Goods entered institutions virtually unable to share and develop them because so much of their capacities were aimed inward, especially toward the hard work of isolating and differentiating themselves—including the extra-hard work of repressing the human drive to mate and form families.

I do not mean to offend the celibate religious of the present era with their ethic of service and their insistence that their calling is meant only for a few special, carefully tested individuals. But I do narrow my eyes at the pious medieval fortresses. By their nature, the contribution these institutions could make to holding society together in difficult times was limited. As a Classicist, I know of their role in preserving pagan learning, to be rediscovered during the Renaissance and later, but contemporary society outside could have used the books that monastic orders, as often as not, stockpiled and left to rot.

Robin Lane Fox includes in *Augustine: Conversions to Confessions* a parallel biography of the contemporary bishop, Synesius, whom I mentioned earlier. This learned estate owner was recruited to head the church in another major North African city, Ptolemais. Celibacy was not yet required for clergymen, and he held out against it. As head of a traditional elite household, Synesius took charge of military responses to dangerous incursions. (Augustine had to bargain with traffickers to try to secure the release of kidnapped and enslaved peasants.) Synesius educated his children. (Augustine, after Adeodatus's death, no longer cared as much about the cultivation of young intelligence even for religious purposes and tended to argue that basic literacy and numeracy would do for the faithful.) Synesius could employ skills learned in a previous career of far-flung diplomacy. (Augustine had foregone politics and a statesman's career in foregoing marriage. An energetic and dedicated interest in public life was for family men; it was connected to their household leadership.) Synesius also would have presided over a business network, while his wife would have helped keep order in their household. In this domain, how to treat the sick; how to prevent or quell quarrels; how to inculcate manners, morals, and skills; and how to acquire and distribute food and clothing were not problems that required a rigid new set of rules and minute supervision to be laid out in a wordy document. No, the household was (if not a gentle and equitable institution) an age-old way of life whose solidity left plenty of energy for other ventures.

The facts suggest that sidelining the household and the nuclear family was not the church's best idea. Violence, ignorance, disorganization, squalor, and the collapse of useful rules in favor of superstitious rituals were the main ingredients of Dark Age dystopia. Without women able to stand in the way with their traditional authority rooted in the sovereign household, Europe took on the culture of a frat house, with men working things out on their own the way they tend to work things out on their own. As the next chapter will show, once the independent status of the family is undermined, bad things can happen that were unimaginable before.

CHAPTER 4

HAMMERED

*A Monk Off His Head About
Women's Bodies*

During the witch hunts of the early modern period, defendants—the great majority of them women—were targeted by personal enemies, gossipy neighbors, churchmen, and state officials. The accused were jailed and often tortured during their "testing," which had a relentless objective: their utter humiliation if not their destruction. The absurdity of the famous witch trial scene in *Monty Python and the Holy Grail* hits the nail on the head. A bellowing half-wit mob that brings a young woman to a purported expert will not contemplate any outcome other than burning her alive. The expert's goal is the same, but he insists on a pretext of cerebral restraint. His questioning of the mob elicits the conclusion that if the woman weighs the same as a duck, she is a witch. His own "largest scales" confirm that she does, and off to the pyre she goes. Witch-hunting was an enterprise in which intellectual and state authority teamed up to put abysmal bigotry into sadistic action.

Women already occupied a theologically justified low status that was interpreted to their great disadvantage. Augustine proudly reports that his mother, rendered properly submissive by God, used to tell her friends that they had no grounds for complaining about the bruises their husbands inflicted, because their marriage contracts reduced them to slavery; their beatings were their own fault for not catering to their husbands' foul moods, the way she did.[1] This Christian attitude that women deserved to suffer bore ugly legal and societal fruit throughout the centuries to come.

But the institutional Catholic Church itself, with its celibate leaders, had the greatest scope for legalized tyranny over women. Its power was international and based on a lively fear of excommunication and hell as punishments for disobedience. Popes commanded their own armies, and what they lacked in international military reach beyond Italy, they made up for in their ability to requisition forces from all over Europe. In 1095, Pope Urban II instigated the first crusade with a sermon. As for capital, its sheer amount made the pope a sort of co-ruler in every kingdom in Europe: Churches, monasteries, and universities had substantial tax revenue as well as income-generating property of their own. The church made and enforced laws for itself, and it reached beyond itself by regulating secular life under the aegis of church or canon law.

When the Protestant Reformation and the Renaissance brought serious challenges to the church's power, the Catholic authorities were ready and able to react ferociously, with measures such as the suppression of Anabaptist governance in Münster (1535–36), when the bodies of dissenting leaders, tortured and executed, were displayed outdoors in cages, and the trial of Galileo (1633), in which he recanted his scientific observations under threat of torture.

Starting in the late fifteenth century, the church also began to devote new resources to persecuting women specifically. Official Christian misogyny was of course longstanding, but it is easy to see why the Vatican saw women as a special threat to its ambitions to control communities that stirred restlessly against the restrictions of doctrinaire Catholicism. Part of this threat was economic. Women with their practical and material interests in the home naturally competed with clerical influence toward investment in life after death (which, in practical terms, meant in the church), rather than in life that continued down the generations. Women were "worldly"; they recruited able young men to secular life, to a lifetime of working and earning for their families and treating religious obligations as secondary.

In this connection, there was a solid rationale in the witch trials that the Vatican and its Inquisition[2] organized in Central Europe, beginning a reign of terror that spread over the continent and continued sporadically for more than three hundred years. The body count for witch-hunting was somewhere in the tens of thousands, and was about eighty percent female.[3]

The witch-hunters were unrestrained by the realities of evidence, as the crime of witchcraft was something that did not exist and so could be prosecuted and punished on any made-up pretext. If a husband was impotent; if a woman miscarried; if she chose the wrong midwife or the wrong friends; if she was too pretty or outspoken or had a curious mole; if a woman was a midwife herself, or in any other way a healer or helper of fertile women, and especially if anything went wrong with one of them, she could find herself in jail and on trial. It looks very much like a persecution of women as such, or like a persecution of women in connection to fertility and childbirth.

Secular and church law—both of which drew on well-developed Roman law—were supposed to allow for the honest pursuit of a just verdict. Until the late fifteenth century, in fact, European legal systems did not work particularly well for trying witches; there tended to be too much doubt available around alleged magical crimes, and even successful prosecutions could look terrible. Joan of Arc's conviction as a witch, and her burning by foreign occupiers, only improved her posthumous reputation. Witch-hunters faced so much skepticism from the public and from fellow clerics that they could not make much headway until they turned *skepticism* about witchcraft into a crime and vigorously threatened death for it.

What exactly, then, gave the early modern witch hunts their specially virulent motivation? The background is complex, but a few influences would be difficult to dispute. Witch-hunting's heyday began in the near run-up to the Protestant Reformation. The papacy had been challenged for centuries by dissident sects and individuals and battered by wars with neighboring states and internal corruption and conflict.[4] At the same time, the church contended with increasingly sophisticated and self-confident lay communities. These communities were making use of new technologies—critical among which was the printing press. New trade routes had opened and new sources of secular learning had become accessible—ironically, this had been made possible mainly through the crusades that were meant to subdue the known world to Catholic authority. In response, the Inquisition became increasingly active in finding evidence of resistance to doctrinaire Catholicism and bringing offenders into line.

During the latter half of the fifteenth century, the papacy and the Inquisition, when they intensified witchcraft persecutions, went a critical step further. Officials formally prioritized a purge not of provable offenses (for example, reading forbidden books and teaching forbidden ideas) but instead of secret, mystical associations and magical acts. The resulting combination of superstition, hearsay, pseudoscience, pseudophilosophy, and pseudotheology, elaborated and transferred to the legal realm as a weapon, was important in the development of totalitarianism. A much more relentless probing of thoughts, personal relationships, and private activities was licensed than ever before, and the information obtained was twisted and falsified to justify the imposition of an entire nightmare world on those who resisted authority or just accidentally got in its way.

It seems far-fetched that such an extreme campaign could succeed. Yet witch-hunting proved in some ways sturdier than the Catholic church itself, and squirmed away, found new lairs, and throve clear through the Reformation and after it, sometimes under Protestant regimes. The torture methods became highly specialized, and came to include "pricking," or stabbing all over the body (with a preference for the private parts) with a dedicated ice pick–like instrument, which on its own killed some of the accused.

Witch-hunting was not a wholly unique abuse; it shared ideas, language, and techniques with the persecution of Jews, and in fact the culminating campaign against these prior to the twentieth century, the Spanish Inquisition, started about the same time, in 1478, also lasted more than three centuries, also spread to the New World, and—as its name indicates—was carried out by the same agency, which drew its authority from the Vatican. A classic of anti-Semitism, called the *Malleus Iudaeorum* or *A Hammer Against Jews*, was published in 1420, and the *Malleus Maleficarum* or (literally) *A Hammer Against Evil-Doing Women* in 1486.[5]

One common feature of both witch-hunting and the persecution of Jews is intimate targeting *within* a society. The Jews—and Muslims—the Inquisition pursued were a fixture of Spanish society, deeply assimilated, and easily trapped in the suddenly undertaken persecution because they expected to be tolerated under the new Christian ascendency for their many positive contributions, for example, to trade, the professions, and learned culture. Defying—and in fact exploiting—this sense of belonging, Catholic officials targeted families that included Christian converts, spied within neighborhoods and households, and tortured loved ones in front of each other. Witch-hunting also targeted well-established people—primarily midwives and fertile wives—and turned their trusted private relationships against them. Patients, medical attendants, husbands, friends, and blood relatives could inform on them falsely or go down horribly along with them. This too was a campaign that kicked down the stubborn boundaries between public and private life and aimed to leave no one feeling safe.

Witch-hunting was at first concentrated in the German-speaking principalities, which were duchies like Saxony and Bavaria and a number of other realms. The Vatican had singled out this relatively divided and thus vulnerable region to bleed with the mass sale of indulgences—certificates that promised the remission of divine punishment in the afterlife, the more expensive indulgences, of course, covering the weightier sins.

Though England's Henry VIII famously rejected the Catholic Church and began persecuting Catholics because the pope would not allow him to divorce one queen and acquire another, serious-minded reformers like Martin Luther found their most popular, most effective Catholic target for criticism in the shakedown carnivals traveling in Central Europe. A cleric could exchange hundreds of pieces of paper for pounds of coin in a single day in a single city after a rousing sermon, but the spectacle soon got old and ugly to all classes of locals, who watched their wealth drain off to Rome in this way. Theological and political pushback was inevitable, and Rome pushed back in turn by ratcheting up repression, most brutally by witch-hunting. The leading instigator of the persecution during this time, Heinrich Kramer, was—not coincidentally, I think—a (reportedly corrupt) seller of indulgences, as well as a habitué of throwing his clerical weight around at every other opportunity, but with a distinct preference for harassing women.

Kramer's popular guide, the *Hammer Against Evil-Doing Women,* is a monument not only to his own vicious ingenuity but to the marshalling of resources for witch-hunting by the papacy, the Inquisition, and the universities that were under church control. Kramer and the coauthor later claimed for the book, Jacob Sprenger, were both Dominican monks, inquisitors as well as university scholars. The book cites an explicit license from the pope to prosecute witches, and both authors would have had the scholarly background they needed to formulate rationales in the familiar terms of theology, scripture, and church law.

This makes the campaign sound cerebral and calculated, and in part it was, but it seems to have drawn particular viciousness from the emotional provocation ordinary women stood to provide. Celibate male Catholic religious had always been alienated from women, whom they had vowed not to touch and whom they were trained to regard as walking temptations, daughters of the arch-traitor Eve. But women of the high-medieval period benefitted significantly from the increasing wealth, culture, and mobility available in Europe, and they must have offered a particularly poignant provocation through their new confidence and assertiveness.

In the German-speaking region, the Fugger banking establishment of Bavarian Augsburg was emblematic of the rise of the burgher—the solid, well-to-do citizen whose sense of his place in the world didn't depend on religion. He wasn't a nobleman from an ancient family that was said to rule with a mandate from God or an illiterate, overworked peasant who was told to accept his lowly station because God had put him in it and who could look to the church's charity if he were sick or starving. The burgher might feel that he had built or maintained his own comfortable perch in the world. Beside the burgher was the burgher's wife: well-fed, well-dressed, canny, literate, managing the household in such a way as to enhance her husband's commercial establishment and his public position. She wasn't at the bottom of the social heap like a poor peasant woman, and she wasn't like the noblewoman who was largely limited to the role of marital pawn and dynastic breeder. Bourgeois women were apparently less impressed than others were with the clergy and bolder in expressing their views. Silent, marginal women, particularly the poor and single mothers, proved vulnerable to witch-hunting, but it was well-placed housewives who seem to have primarily attracted attention in the era of more intense witch-hunting. In overwhelming numbers, the documented victims are married or widows—that is, not servile or outcast women but women presiding over their own homes.[6]

Kramer, in fact, had a run-in with one such woman and lost, which apparently stung like the dickens. Helena Scheuberin of Innsbruck, the wife of a well-off citizen, sounds like a Wife of Bath type. Chaucer's vivid, outspoken character in *The Canterbury Tales* is riding off on a pilgrimage on her own, after she has maneuvered her husband into renouncing his clerical-derived misogyny and turning the management of his property over to her. Scheuberin seems to have publicly reviled Kramer's paranoid sermonizing. Kramer then prosecuted Scheuberin and her supporters, but with such insouciance about due process that the local bishop stepped in. Kramer, who would not give up digging for dirt to incriminate the group, to the bishop's exasperation, was eventually induced to leave town.

Then, it appears, Kramer the scholar, monk, and involuntarily rusticated inquisitor worked diligently to complete the *Hammer Against Evil-Doing Women*; Sprenger's role (if any) as a coauthor was likely minor. The project, however, was not just Kramer's personal furious screed; it had clearly found university and Vatican sympathy. In the front matter are endorsements of learned theologians and the recent papal bull authorizing a witch-hunting crackdown. At any rate, though, the book reeks of the obsessive misogyny that a man not at peace with his celibacy is apt to manifest. Here is a typical passage:

> [A generic woman's] walk, bearing, and demeanor—this is the vanity of vanities. There is no man in the world who strives to please Beneficent God as much as even a woman who is moderate in her vanities strives to please men.... Again, she is "more bitter than death" [Ecclesiastes 7:26] because the death of the body is an open, fearsome

enemy, but woman is a hidden, cajoling one, and for this reason she is more bitter and dangerous. She is called a snare of hunters, that is, of demons, because men are captured not merely through carnal desires at the sight and sound of them ... but also through their affecting countless men and domestic animals with sorcery.[7]

In other words, the creature whose very presence agonizes men (like me) is necessarily malicious and destructive. Since there is no clear *sign* of her bad intentions or acts—she is, on the contrary, attending Mass in modest clothes, or going to the market to buy food for her family—she must be up to *secret* evil in collusion with *secret* beings.

The chief of the *Hammer*'s accusations, that women mated with demons and produced demonic offspring and that they killed babies and dedicated them to Satan, have a nexus with this same perverted reasoning. The most dutiful, self-sacrificial, and constructive thing women could do was to conceive, bear, and nurture children. Their discipleship to the faultless, holy mother Mary was routine and plain to see. But a cleric with an unbreakable will to hate and persecute women would see this virtuous calling to motherhood as an abominable *deception*.

Neurotic personal agendas aside, however, targeting young wives and mothers was a brilliant political strategy at a time when the Catholic Church wished to threaten and cow a restless, rising class of its members, the bourgeoisie. Stepped-up witch-hunting allowed clerics to rip open the heart of the bourgeois home and greatly disrupt the lives of people who were increasingly able to rely on their own resources and their own experience of what was good for them, and who were thus increasingly skeptical of the uses the church made of its power. Moreover, going after women for atrocities alleged to have happened in the most private circumstances (with few or no actual witnesses beyond the midwives who were prone to being co-accused) rendered defense extremely difficult and made the process itself the punishment. Prolonged humiliation was unavoidable, no matter how a case turned out. To put it in terms of the bleakest facts, women, and sometimes even young girls, were summarily hauled away, pitilessly interrogated, tortured, maimed, defamed, and killed, and their families were left to bear the damage for generations. The natural impulse for women and their loved ones to resist to the utmost would have met with a vicious threat: Resistance was itself a crime against the church.

Of course, such a policy signaled an unwillingness to let the judicial system operate in the age-old way, with both prosecution and defense free to do their jobs, and those who knew and respected the law were alarmed. But Kramer seems to have been a classic populist authoritarian in that he talked over the heads of responsible people and persuaded oafs and opportunists to move fast and break things. And like Hitler, history's most successful populist authoritarian, he had a wordy and pompous book to herald his program.

When I started to research and outline a book on fertility-related misogyny, I didn't think of covering *The Hammer Against Evil-Doing Women*, though I knew it was the most important guide for prosecuting witches. I had in mind the typical modern notion of witches as either ugly cackling crones or beautiful demonic vamps, and it took me some time to find out that when witch-hunting was on the upswing, witches were identified mainly as married mothers and midwives. To the influential

Kramer, childbearing capacity was plainly an obsession, and the alleged perversions of this capacity were the main rationale for his campaign. For him and other witch-hunters, the erotic elements in witchcraft were important because of their alleged reproductive results: Women were mating with demons and breeding Satan's army. At the same time, women and their midwives were destroying husbands' offspring through abortion and infanticide, or else dedicating newborns to hellish purposes. In these turbulent times, people worried about the apocalypse happening imminently, so witch-hunters could scarily invoke the possibility of God's opponents becoming a huge and powerful contingent—though this is surely one of the weirder manifestations of male size anxiety in all of history.

Really and truly, the witch-hunting cosmological narrative as it now emerged was meant to inspire a demographic panic. I could compare the narrative to the emperor Augustus's fearmongering about Roman women's alleged low fertility, or American fearmongering about the peril to economic competitiveness, or to the white race, or to Western civilization (especially Christianity) if the right women do not pony up larger broods. But in the endgame "logic" of witch-hunting, the fate of not one nation, group, or culture could appear to be at risk but the fate of the universe. This was the ultimate justification (or pretext) for the ferocious concentration of the *Hammer*—and of the investigations and prosecutions it inspired—on pregnancy, childbirth, and the care of newborns.

This is self-evident in the lengthy first part of the *Hammer* outline with which Christopher Mackay helpfully precedes his translation of the dense and complex text. Kramer's argument for the urgency of the judicial procedures through which he is about to guide his readers centers on women's reproductive crimes in collaboration with demons. The author gets right down to the points (as Mackay phrases them): "Demons necessarily cooperate with sorceress" and "Demons beget humans to increase number of sorceresses." Kramer moves on to accuse women of impeding procreation, removing penises, and killing fetuses and newborns. He discusses nonsexual female crimes, but the thrust of his indictment is clear: Women commit outrages against natural reproduction. No wonder Kramer argues that sorcery—the special kind of magic with which he is concerned—is worse than the fall of the demons, or the change of some angels into demonic enemies of God and their expulsion from heaven into hell.[8]

The earliest editions of the *Hammer* are not illustrated, but illustrations appear starting about a generation later, and many of them reflect the fever-dream of lost, stolen, and corrupted fertility. For example, one engraving shows four people—it is unclear to me whether they are male or female but their jutting chins may mark them as older women—eagerly passing two infants to a coal-black, horned, winged, grinning devil, who extends an arm on either side to receive the offerings.

For all of its fantastical, mushroom-trip atmosphere, the *Hammer* is not a particularly original work. It draws on existing ideas and authority, from sources as old as Hebrew scripture and as new as contemporary Catholic dogma and decrees. It was not even the first high-medieval guide to witchcraft. But its combination of titillation and horror in the stories about women as the intimate enemy within human society helped make the book a sensation. For the sake of comparison, the Gutenberg Bible was famous and sought-after, but fewer than two hundred copies were produced in a single edition from the new movable-type printing press during the early 1450s; between 1486 and 1600, twenty-eight editions of the *Hammer* appeared, according to Wikipedia. Exact numbers of copies are not of course known, but this was clearly one of the most prolific early printed books, intended from the start to be a blockbuster. First editions are still so common that leading antique dealers have offered them for five-figure prices. You would need to add at least one zero to buy a first-edition *Don Quixote*.[9]

The *Hammer* may have had a shaping influence on misogyny in the West, especially on the hysterical, paranoid treatment of women's fertility. Kramer shows a striking genius for depicting the worst evildoing imaginable in every scenario in this realm, but something is familiar in his twisted mindset: Women must reproduce, and while they do, they need the most stringent policing to prevent and punish their reproductive crimes. Kramer gives, for example, a gloating account of a husband who was devastated to discover, by spying during his child's birth, that both his wife and teenage daughter were witches. The daughter was serving as her mother's midwife and may have used a strap in some way the father did not understand, perhaps to help in the delivery or to suspend the newborn for weighing. In any case, the father claimed the strap was a magical device for holding up the baby not by human but by demonic agency. Maybe the whole thing was a setup, and the accuser had a girlfriend waiting for the marital bed. Whatever went on, it would have been his wife and daughter's word against his. He conscientiously contrived "proof" of their witchcraft, and then turned them in; and they were burned, the poor man.[10]

Over time, judicial processes along the lines of those the *Hammer* prescribes normalized such victimization and established the propriety of visiting the full fury of religious zealotry on women in their most private and vulnerable roles—a great change from the earlier medieval status quo. Many celibate male Christian authors had been fierce misogynists without going over the edge and resorting to active persecution of women as women, a prospect that readily throws up objections in any normal mind. It is a challenging business to terrorize woman and control them completely while still extracting offspring from them under the guise of beneficent male authority. This is the dilemma that informs Margaret Atwood's *Handmaid's Tale*, and before the late fifteenth century, there doesn't seem to have been much appetite for pursuing a solution.

Witch-hunting inquisitors seem to have been the first people to address themselves fearlessly to the problem, and in their solutions, they landed somewhere between the punishment fetishist and the incel who murders women he can't have. This attitude and conduct on the part of religious leaders would have been shocking in any age and needed a very special kind of packaging. This included a modern type of propagandistic repetition and absurdity, a beating senseless through language. The authorial voice in the *Hammer* never stops trying to screen the reader's view of what he is actually thinking and feeling and why, and this effort results in some of the worst writing in publication history. Or maybe the terrible writing is on some level deliberate: The words punish anyone trying to find coherence in them.

Western politics has always depended inordinately on language, and especially on justifying power through writing. This tendency was aggravated in Christianity, with its stress on abstract and invisible authority meant to replace gods representing evident natural forces and human impulses and worshipped as solid effigies. The transcendent Word at the beginning of the Gospel of John was now in charge, and it spread its influence through scripture, which is literally "writing." Scholasticism, the leading means of expounding theology during the Middle Ages, gives a certain sense of language presiding in isolation, of the guy with the most confident Latin lording it over everybody else. Scholasticism presented short, prefab questions (like the ones in the modern catechism, which is influenced by this methodology), and windily "proved" things like what God intended in creating humankind. But at least the leading Scholastic author, Thomas Aquinas, used Aristotle, a real logician and natural scientist, in ways that were not altogether laughable. Witch-hunting literature, and the *Hammer* in particular, takes Scholasticism and doses it with intellectual anthrax, with absurd assertions and a misused mishmash of older authority, particularly pagan classical authors, scripture, and the Church Fathers.

In some respects, this misuse utterly defies the religious tradition. On the subject of malicious wagging tongues, for example, scripture speaks with a single voice of censure. A whole book of the biblical Apocrypha—Susanna—is devoted to a story about lustful liars who connive to haul an innocent woman up on a capital charge of adultery but suffer the death penalty themselves when Daniel proves their guilt by a clever interrogation. The chief "evidence" that the *Hammer* touts is imaginative hearsay, and above all sexual gossip, the most poisonous kind of talk that neighborhoods tend to ooze, with subject matter so private yet so consequential that it provides an easy means for the ruin of the blameless. This is the hinge on which the plot of Susanna turns: Elders ambush a beautiful young wife who has stripped to bathe in her own walled garden, and because she will not have sex with them, they claim to have caught her in flagrante delicto with someone else.

The *Hammer* positively touts unexamined testimony on such sensitive matters. Mere gossip is not only not condemned; it is to be the substance of prosecutions. It is literally prescribed that people be arrested and tried on the charge of having a "bad reputation," whether what has been said against them is trivial or serious or ridiculous. To make things worse, only evidence of well-motivated enmity on the part of accusers can set the accused free. And apparently this evidence cannot compete with other evidence and win out, but must stand alone. There must be no harm to children or livestock that can be laid at the accused's feet, no general rumor, no other witnesses against her, nothing. Everything that *can* count against her *must* count against her.

A guide to prosecution, including a typology of various accusations according to how weighty they are and procedural instructions for each gradation of case, is almost two hundred pages long in Mackay's translation, but it all shamelessly weighs toward arbitrary cruelty. None of the accused, it seems, must escape the lengthiest process and the maximum torment possible. If proof of a negative is forced down the court's throat and the definitively blameless accused cannot be tormented any longer, she must still listen to a "sentence" full of pious prosecutorial self-justification. And she must be subject to another arrest and trial at the drop of a hat. The *Hammer* sternly warns against the appearance of exoneration. Modern constitutional law bans double jeopardy for a reason. It used to be a favorite game of judicial abusers.

The prosecutors, it is understood, can err only by not pushing hard enough for convictions, and so they have virtual carte blanche. Demonic protection, on the other hand, is a pretext for stripping the accused of traditional recourses. They must be denied even the old superstitious trial by ordeal, chiefly because, if a woman seems to show her innocence by carrying a red-hot iron in her hand for several paces, it could just be a demonic trick. Likewise, if she holds out under torture and does not confess, this does not rule out her guilt, as witches are known to achieve immunity from pain through the "sorcery of silence." By the way, a victim of judicial torture must be carefully guarded so that she does not kill herself—which would be the fault of the devil (not the torturer). Inquisitors are instructed on how to chase the fun clear to the end without incurring any guilt or shame: Turn over the victims to the civil authorities to be burned alive, but with a tender plea to spare them bodily harm. Of course, if they did spare them, there would be hell to pay. The plea was meant merely as a sort of magic spell of self-exoneration.

The *Hammer*'s attitude toward women (the book discusses men's sorcery, which is related mainly to weapons, in just a few pages) is not only obsessive, it is lunatic. A merely neurotic person may fixate on germs or the dangers of flying, or, with fear or disgust, may shun cats, or men, or women, but can recognize the attitude as personal and will not demand that it govern the world. In the *Hammer*, overexcited suspicions about women are not so confined; they are more like a psychosis, whose sufferer is not able to admit that any right-thinking, informed person can disagree about the perils at hand.

I think the hallucinating panic and the sloppy argumentation of the *Hammer* are connected. Lunatics gabble; they are dug deep into their delusions and are not interested in responsive dialogue with people who do not share them. But political lunatics can be cunning in their communications; they can be good at the particular nonsense that appeals to their audience. Hitler was good at congenial blather in *Mein Kampf*, and good at a congenial rage in his rally speeches. Kramer was good at sounding coherently learned and reasonable in a world where an education that lasted more than a few years was rare and one that allowed a critical, objective view of other people's learning was pretty much nonexistent. He was also a virtuoso in the kind of lurid gossip he licensed as the basis of prosecutions; if he had lived in our time, he might have been a successful horror screenwriter. He tells of a woman who defecated thorns and bones and pieces of wood under a curse from a midwife with whom she had quarreled. He claims that a midwife was caught dropping a newborn baby's severed arm from a bundle in public and confessed under torture to infanticides "without number." The wife whose husband raped her and then expressed a gloating hope that he had impregnated her is supposed to have meant her retort, "May that fruit be given to the Devil," literally. A peasant finds out that his wife, corrupted by demons, has taught his eight-year-old daughter to bring down rain instantly on one field at a time; he has his wife convicted and burned and his daughter rebaptized.[11]

Through these modes, Kramer managed to bring the blaming of women to a shrieking pitch of intensity, but he did not alienate or disgust his public, who kept right on buying and reading his book and tolerating the witch trials it helped inspire. As Europe headed out of the era of the crusades, when the rage and greed of Christianity fell on Islam, and into an era of devastating conflict between factions of Christians, culminating in the notorious Thirty Years' War of 1618–1648, the great villain, according to Kramer, was not the man with a mace or a pike or his ruthless leader, but a married woman having babies and the nurses and healers who did their best to help her.

And it was of course not only emotions that he stoked, but an actual widespread if episodic persecution. Such exuberantly sadistic treatment of women, never in a single instance avenged, must have suggested that women could and should bear anything, and set them up as a huge class of go-to scapegoats. It had been demonstrated, after all, that sadistic thugs masquerading as religious and moral leaders and an absurdist excuse for a legal system could make a busy show of prosecuting women's imaginary crimes and ignore men's actual, habitual, heinous ones: of violence, of corruption, of foreign rampages and local oppression. The lesson was that, while men could run amok because they were men, women must be punished for being women.

The pattern is not alien, I insist, to one way in which current American crises are being addressed. We have out-of-control greed on a planet with shrinking resources, we have whopping fiscal, moral, and institutional deficits—and there is a wild alacrity in some quarters in shunting women and their wombs into sole responsibility for the state of our society. In Maine, a state legislator blamed a mass shooting on liberalized access to abortion. When challenged, he doubled down.[12] He was following an established American formula: Abortion reduces respect for life and thus promotes other crimes and vices, and God's punishments fall on such a wicked nation. As alleged centuries before, the only really important set of crimes, the fountainhead of evil, is female.

The inquisitors' deafness to their victims' various pleas is akin to right-wing American politicians' indifference to whether a particular woman has had a miscarriage or an abortion when she shows up in the emergency room and asks for medical care; whether a fetus potentially subject to termination is healthy or going to perish naturally at any moment; whether it is in its first or its eighth month of development; whether a "mother" is even pregnant or just inseminated, and no ovum has been fertilized and implanted; whether she had sex willingly or was brutally raped. The dismissal of these questions is not a bug in the system. It is a feature—a feature covered up with endless fact-averse words. The feature is implacable persecution. Women, like the accused in witch trials, are not supposed to have a means of escape; if they could argue their case, if they could be justly exonerated and walk free, then male responsibility for the state of the world would begin to become devastatingly plain by contrast.

CHAPTER 5

HELL'S BELLS

Dickens Shills for Victorian Misery

IF ANYONE SHOULD HAVE LACKED A BLIND SPOT ABOUT fertility in newly industrialized Britain, it was Charles Dickens (1812–1870). He was the second of eight children, and before his siblings were even all born, his father went to debtors' prison and the twelve-year-old son was dispatched to work in a boot blacking factory.[1] After his episodic schooling ended at the age of fifteen, he went to work as a solicitor's office boy. For his entire life, Dickens brooded over his parents' careless treatment of him, and it virtually created him as a public figure. His heartrending portrayals of neglected, abandoned, exploited, and immiserated children reached the very rare status of classics influential enough to inspire parodies that are classics in their turn, such as Gilbert and Sullivan's *Pirates of Penzance* and the Miles Cowperthwaite sketches on *Saturday Night Live*.[2]

But the waifs in Dickens's stories are loners as a rule, without siblings (although an orphaned brother and sister come of age in *Nicholas Nickleby*). They arise from all kinds of circumstances but never from a couple having more children than they can comfortably support, or more than they have any sustained interest in as individuals. In the case of Dickens's family, it was both. The father was a government clerk with a modest income, and he prioritized a showy social life over providing for all his children's future.

Dickens was unwilling to face these facts head-on through his fiction; instead, he reflected the joys of his upbringing in a large family. He adored his older sister—even though, in sharp contrast to his own educational fate, she attended an elite musical academy—and he greatly enjoyed the expensive festivities to which his father was addicted. Family affection and family celebrations, the more the merrier, get excellent press in his novels. The psychology of denial (a natural impulse of ill-used children) may help explain why he does not also depict the *disadvantages* of a large family with limited resources, as Jane Austen had quite ruthlessly done with the Prices in *Mansfield Park* (1814), and why he in fact presents a strained, over-the-top impression that many children make a home, however poor, merry, affectionate, and hopeful.

In forming his own family, certainly, Dickens quite evidently did what those misused during childhood tend to do. He tried to force a different ending on what was basically the same story. Dickens married at twenty-four, three days after he published the first installment of his first novel, *The Pickwick Papers*, and rather quickly had ten children, nine of whom survived infancy (there were also two or more miscarriages). He replicated the size of his childhood household, and then some. Keeping up with the bills was a high-wire act, and he was personally as obtuse and neglectful as his father had been (he also shared his father's hypocrisy in depicting himself as a benign, put-upon household head). Luckily for everyone, Dickens was a wildly popular writer, not a struggling clerk. He could avoid bringing penury down on his household. But at least his father hadn't deliberately broken up the family. Dickens put aside his wife, even publicly and falsely alleging that she was insane. He isolated her from her children (only the eldest, Charles, continued to live with her) so that he could pursue a secret long-term liaison with a young actress, Ellen Ternan, with whom he probably had two stillborn babies.[3]

Many quirks in Dickens's behavior toward his children suggest that he never saw them as flesh-and-blood human beings, inhabiting the real world and not a fanciful literary one. He gave them names and nicknames that linked them to characters in his novels ("Dora," "Chickenstalker," and the like), to fellow authors ("Edward Bulwer Lytton," for example), and to himself ("Charles Culliford Boz"; Boz was Dickens's pen name). He reacted with startled irritation when they behaved like living babies and children—making noise, requiring attention, having persistently individual problems and needs. His apparent genius for botching their education and adult prospects—a surprising percentage of the boys ended up crashing and burning in distant exile, and just one of the two surviving girls married—smacks of underhand and belated punishment. Overall, he looks like a dismal parent. A more self-aware and candid man would have taken in the evidence of his relationship with his first two or three children when they were tiny and concluded that parenthood was not a congenial calling for him; Dickens just kept the babies coming.

Obvious objections to this criticism of him are that there weren't many ready or appealing alternatives to marriage in Victorian society, and that married couples were challenged in limiting their families (though over time they managed much better than previous generations). The age of undisturbed networks of "wise women"—midwives and herbalists who might provide contraception and abortion—was long over. The witch hunts and the rise of a male medical establishment had stripped the women who cared for other women of much of their old autonomy and authority and sidelined them to the fullest extent possible, much to the detriment of families.

The insensitivity of male doctors to women's reproductive needs is shown, for example, by the practice of having women laboring to give birth lie on their backs instead of sitting in a birthing chair, kneeling, squatting, or standing with support, positions that bring gravity and leverage to the task of expelling the fetus; these were popular choices for women and midwives over the eras when the mechanics of birth were up to them. Male doctors normalized horizontal birth for their own convenience and control. It is easy to suspect that the paradigm was a surgeon working on an unconscious patient or an anatomist cutting up a dead one. No wonder that the vogue for caesarean sections grew enormously in modern medicine in spite of all the disadvantages to both the mother and baby when the operation isn't actually needed.

Nineteenth-century doctors could cite new laws, chiefly those enacted in 1803, 1837, and 1861, to support the extra control they claimed over women's reproductive health. Abortion could now be punished as murder, with sentences of death and lifetime penal servitude. The distinction between pregnancy before and after "quickening," or the first fetal movements a woman can perceive, was eventually removed, opening up the possibility of punishing abortion from the time of conception. Anyone who assisted in an abortion, including through the procurement of drugs, could also be liable. Such laws were a powerful deterrent to the supply of contraceptives; at this stage of medical knowledge, there was no clear distinction between the workings of contraception and abortion where mere insemination or very early pregnancy was concerned.

Also working against women's and couples' reproductive autonomy was a new regimen of prudery that deprived women of the awareness and knowledge of their intimate bodies and those of men. Women weren't supposed even to think about the processes that generated new life. Everything served to obfuscate, from the new voluminousness of skirts to new conversational taboos. But at the same time, more people of both sexes were traveling and working outside the home and family than ever; urbanization and commercialization were rife, adding to young people's exposure. Victorian *society* was more open and mobile, and thus more sexually risky, even while the spread of sexual *information* was discouraged.

At the same time, however, the eighteenth-century vogue of sensibility, the Romantic movement, and Victorian sentimentality had brought changes in customs that were helpful in limiting families. The right to some autonomy in courtship and a freer choice of a wedding date were more and more widely sanctioned, so there was an obvious way for couples to limit their family size according to their own ideas of what was suitable: delayed marriage. The longer a pair of sweethearts waited, the smaller the size of their eventual family.

They in fact had plenty of traditional authority for this, based on the longstanding principle of "prudence." The squalid, uproarious, neglectful Price household in Jane Austen's Regency novel *Mansfield Park*, the result of a young, impetuous marriage and too many children, points out the horrors of the defiant "imprudence" that nearly all Austen's other fictional couples avoid. The well-rooted Victorian establishment did not judge differently. A letter from the Reverend Dodgson to his son Charles (whom we know as Lewis Carroll), when Charles was twenty-three and about to be appointed Mathematical Lecturer at Oxford, urges him to save and invest £150 a year (including premiums on a life insurance policy) for ten years, at the end of which he can responsibly "settle."[4] The reverend had eleven children himself, and until he got a more lucrative post, his financial worries were acute. He had lost a wife in what should have been her prime, and he was head of a house full of unmarried daughters who could not respectably venture into independence. He clearly thought that thirty-three was not too old for his brilliant son to wed; an important but unspoken benefit of that wait would be a less exhausting, less expensive family.

A corollary to this thinking was widely embraced at the time: The destitute should not marry at all. Writers in the new field of political economy noted the connection between a growing population of the unskilled poor and wage-gouging. Any visitor to an urban industrial slum could see the havoc wrought by many closely spaced births in an exploited community, where mothers might have to chase starvation wages while burdened with babies and toddlers, and where older children were left to their own devices or dispatched to work themselves. Prolonged or lifelong celibacy was not the easiest sell to the poor, but many thousands of domestic servants put up with it. A spouse and children were not allowed to compete for the energies of a young skivvy or gardener sweating all the daylight hours to care for someone else's home. But a trusted key-holder of many years' standing might marry, and the few (if any) children resulting would not distract unduly from the easier work that was usual at this stage.

Dickens's paternal grandmother was an example. She was a servant who married at thirty-six a well-placed manservant who was considerably older. She had only two children, and did so well by the youngest, the future father of Charles, that he secured a government office job at a time when social mobility was relatively rare. For the young who were unanchored and unskilled, an early love match might be tempting, but if they were smart, they would bear in mind the number of things that could go wrong and the ragged state of the social safety net. The Poor Law Amendment Act of 1834 greatly reduced the scope for "outdoor relief" at public expense (the kind of benefits that we would identify with an ordinary public-welfare system) by consigning the destitute who were deemed able-bodied to large prisonlike workhouses where conditions were designedly harsh and included the forced separation of families and a near-starvation diet. Desperate people were supposed to be terrified of the workhouse, but the government did its best to leave them no other help. It was barbaric, but the older, more generous, and more flexible network of public provisions for the poor could not withstand the restiveness of taxpayers in the face of widespread economic insecurity, which made daunting demands on the fiscus.

Dickens—author, social critic, and philanthropist—did not respect any of these considerations for poor people as they tried to shape lives that were both survivable and fulfilling. In fact, his faith in the benefits of large families in all circumstances amounted to a cultlike religion. Narratively, Dickens tends to come at the large family as a hazily glowing abstraction or a festive stage-set, which had nothing to do with the reality: significant decline in both early marriage and fertility, in part because of the failure of economic expansion to ensure social and material security. The large family is the happy ending toward which most of his plots aim. The only conceivable refuge for his young, virtuous, good-looking protagonists, if they can get through all their bizarre obstacles, is a cozy, full home, the great harbinger of which is a servile, tender, sentimental girl, naive and malleable and strictly home-oriented even though she might have been exposed to many hard knocks. Such is the candidate to become a perfect mother. Mrs. Jellyby in *Bleak House* is a monster of neglect and ruinous extravagance because she is interested in something that takes her outside of her family, namely charity—on which Dickens the family *man* spent a great deal of time and money.

For the large and happy families Dickens depicts, he does not even bother to make narrative arguments, which would require situating the characters amid plausible events and circumstances. Most often, in fact, the full house in question does not even exist on the page. It is a reward that will be bestowed on the most virtuous and lucky characters after the end of the novel. The salvation of existing sizable families tends to be uncanny, even for Dickens, who famously got rid of one character by spontaneous combustion. Mr. Micawber in *David Copperfield* is transformed from a skulking bankrupt, who imagines he can support his wife and children through fast-talking charm, to a pillar of the community when he moves to Australia. (Again, a notable number of Dickens's sons found themselves in far reaches of the Empire, such as the

Yukon, where most did *not* thrive.) The Cratchits in *A Christmas Carol* are delivered from terrible poverty by enchanted dreams.

With his enthusiasm for the happy large family as insistent as it was vaporous, Dickens was the perfect vehicle for fertility propaganda favored by the most powerful people in Britain. Large families just happened to be extremely useful for the industrialists and imperial expansionists who went from commanding in the previous century to an almost sanctified status under Queen Victoria.[5] Slaves and serfs had been overworked and underfed, but they benefitted from their status as *human* capital, not easy to replace because of our species' demanding biology. You could work them to death at a young age, but then where would you find a new supply except through the expensive, risky, laborious plunder of some foreign population?

These were problems that led to such developments as the recognition of Roman slaves as couples entitled to raise children in their own homes. But the industrial revolution encouraged the use of underlings as disposable machine parts. A young mill girl was attached to her loom for most of her waking hours and was not apt to be more docile or dexterous as she grew up, so she might as well be fed on bread that was bulked up with chalk, beaten within an inch of her life if she swooned from exhaustion, and dumped in a pauper's grave when she died—*as long as* there was a replacement at hand from some other desperate family.

The rank-and-file military man, likewise, was not like the selectively recruited, professional Roman legionary or the late-medieval English bowman, whose family belonged to the sturdy yeoman class of farmers. A sailor in the Royal Navy during the Victorian era was a so-called slave, perhaps starting his career by being kidnapped, and he was subject to starvation, torture, rape, and quick disposal in the waves. The infantryman was not much better off. Kipling complains in "The Widow at Windsor" that the soldier's body is an incidental chemical additive, "salt[ing] down" the soil he has agonizingly won: "(Poor beggars!—it's blue with our bones!)"[6]

Victorian—and, particularly, Dickensian—ethics were solidly behind the production of factory and mine and cannon fodder. To yield more people fit for such uses, reproduction needed ideally to be a sentimental and fearful affair, as if the favorite Dickensian plot were real, and all would be well as soon as a couple married; as if anyone who hinted otherwise was an enemy of everything holy and good; and as if the paradise of one's own sweet little home could not, by any stretch of the imagination, take on certain qualities of a battery farm.

This fantasy was hardly unique to Dickens. Its proponent par excellence was the naive, diminutive, smirking young Queen Victoria herself, who bore nine children. Victoria was the loftiest icon of copious motherhood, a new era's revision of the Virgin Mary, who bears and adores only a single child. In reality, Victoria found childbearing a wearing nuisance and left the care and upbringing of her brood largely to servants. But the public imagery of her family was relentless: at the Christmas tree in illustrated weeklies, for example, and arrayed in portraiture on a variety of souvenir tat.

No one could doubt that England's princes and princesses led pleasant lives and would be well provided for; their images represented a celebration of the real domestic comforts gained in Victorian England as the economy and the middle class grew. Dickens's message, aligned with the interests of labor-intensive enterprises such as cotton milling and the repression of insurgency in the

Sudan, could be far more sinister, in effect endorsing pretexts for why those with next to nothing should have large families, with no thought for what would happen to themselves and their children. It was their sacred destiny, it was the only good and hopeful and decent life, Dickens insisted through his stories.

For example, Mr. and Mrs. Cratchit of *A Christmas Carol* have, rationally considered, been "imprudent" to have six children on the scanty salary of a miser's clerk. They can't afford proper care for their disabled child, Tiny Tim, who is fated to die if the Ghosts of Christmas who appear to Ebenezer Scrooge cannot persuade him to become the boy's generous patron. The Cratchits are poignantly, sometimes nervously, jubilant over their Christmas dinner, a rare occasion on which they can leave off work and indulge in meat (a goose) and a dessert (a steamed pudding) and can (with expressions of wonder) eat until they are full. But Dickens trivializes the pitiful limits of their enjoyments. He narratively maneuvers to describe the family feasting with endless satisfaction on each other, as it were, a sort of Pollyanna cannibalism. None of their persistent anxieties and hardships, no element of pathos in this holiday matters because of the delight they draw from one another's company and their adamantine will to see the upside of everything. It is as if the large-mindedness the couple showed in having such a large family is a permanent blessing that makes everyone's burdens light. Mrs. Cratchit hides her eldest daughter (who has left home for some near-imprisoning menial job and has now barely managed to get home after working on Christmas morning) and pretends that she could not come so that the father's joy will be more intense in seeing her again at last. Bob Cratchit is proud to take Tiny Tim to church, though the boy is so weak and so badly handicapped (in the text he has not only a crutch but a metal frame around his body) that he has to be carried home. Tiny Tim has been "[a]s good as gold" and is a living sermon. Bob Cratchit reports: "He told me, coming home, that he hoped the people saw him in the church, because he was a cripple, and it might be pleasant to them to remember upon Christmas Day, who made lame beggars walk, and blind men see."[7]

Tellingly, the male protagonists with whom Dickens identifies closely, those who belong to the middle class by origin or merit, tend to regret any marriage they may enter into in unripe circumstances or with immature judgment—David Copperfield's marriage to Dora, for example, who is *too* empty-headed, or Richard's to Ada in *Bleak House*, which he undertakes while obsessed with a time- and money-wasting lawsuit. These men not only need to marry the perfect woman but to found their homes on assured prosperity. But the poor, according to Dickens, must follow their hearts and let 'er rip. Marriage is the only wholesome outlet for their young energies from the start, not the eventual reward for heroic striving, as for Nicholas Nickleby in the eponymous novel.

In effect, Dickens endorsed the industrial-production model of the family for those who could least endure it. He did not of course explicitly promote the Europe-wide masturbation panic (begun in the eighteenth century with overwrought quack treatises and leading to the use of torture devices that prevented erections, and even clitoridectomies for masturbating girls)[8] to his mixed Victorian audience, but he does tap into the prevailing imagery: Male "solitude" produces a squalid appearance and weakness, illness, madness, addictions—and, without timely intervention, can actually kill the wretched practitioner. But as an all-around Victorian moralist, Dickens abominated *all* sexual outlets that did not produce children. For instance, Little Em'ly in *David Copperfield* runs off with the wicked Steerforth after her marriage with the poor but decent Ham is put off. She returns bereft and broken, to be saved finally by the marriage. The prostitute Nancy in *Oliver Twist* dies in the orphan boy's defense, her mothering instincts pitifully diverted to this purpose.

The extremes to which Dickens will venture to follow his formula that early, fertile marriage averts tragedy for the poor appear most shockingly in "The Chimes." In the novella, the only hope for a whole group of people on the wrong side of subsistence is that two members of the group, a young working woman and a young blacksmith, marry immediately, though he has no prospect of permanent, steady work. Dickens treats the outcomes that would have in reality been probable from the premature start of a family in dire poverty—worse poverty, hardship, exhaustion, despair, illness, and tragedy—as the results of *waiting* to marry.

Dickens was, like Augustine, reacting in part to his own harrowing early experiences. His reactions, also like Augustine's, happened to suit the wishes of a hierarchy in which he gained an influential voice. That doesn't sound like much, but a look at the lengths to which he will go to vindicate his notions as if they were compelling reality, and then a look at his massive cultural influence, give a sobering sense of how much the strange, artificial character of later fertility messaging owes to this one man.

The hero of "The Chimes" is Toby, or "Trotty," Veck, a "ticket porter" or freelance delivery man in London. He is the living notice of his availability, displayed outdoors at all hours and in all weathers in the hope of a job, but his energy and cheerfulness seldom fail. Snow and hail and wind actually nerve him and set him jogging up and down to stay on the alert, notwithstanding that he is so small and frail-looking that he seems in danger of blowing away. Of his physical hardships, only sogginess from rain lowers his mood, as he owns no overcoat or umbrella, and his clothes, shoes, and hat are in a sorry state. He is wistful and a little ironical about his hunger and the luxury he sees around him, but he maintains an upbeat pride: "He loved to earn his money. He delighted to believe—Toby was very poor, and couldn't well afford to part with a delight—that he was worth his salt."[9]

But on New Year's Eve even such a tough and plucky man is downcast from what he reads in a week-old newspaper about the crimes and disasters of the poor: "I get so puzzled sometimes that I am not even able to make up my mind whether there is any good at all in us, or whether we are born bad."[10] The theme of the story is neatly forecast here: Any moral or public-policy strictures against the very poor having many children are an assault on their integrity and their right to exist and do not contain any sincere concern for public welfare; ergo, the way for the very poor to assert their humanity is to marry as soon as possible and depend on a mysterious providence for the support of the large family they will immediately start. This evening Toby is overjoyed at the appearance of his daughter, the twenty-year-old Meg, with her eyes "that reflected back the eyes which searched them; not flashingly, or at the owner's will, but with a clear, calm, honest, patient radiance"; eyes "beautiful and true, and beaming with Hope" despite all the misery they have seen.[11] She brings him a dinner of stewed tripe, teasing him merrily with the shopping basket and making him guess what is in it. But her news does not bring him joy. She and her sweetheart Richard, a blacksmith, have decided to marry the next day, on the strength of his work being secure "for some time to come"; they are afraid that if they continue to wait from year to year until they are better off—and Richard concedes that they will be poor in the future too—they will both die sad and lonely.[12]

But all three—Toby, Meg, and Richard—are cast down by the intrusion of three nosey gentlemen. One is Mr. Filer, an economist who criticizes Toby's tripe as wasteful: It costs too much to produce and so is a wrong way to allocate nourishment to the population at large. Another of the gentlemen (unnamed) is nostalgic for the good old days of the hearty peasantry. Soon Filer's displeasure blazes up to fantastic rhetorical heights at the news that the young couple are to marry:

> "Ah," cried Filer, with a groan. "Put *that* down, indeed, Alderman, and you'll do something. Married! Married! The ignorance of the first principles of political economy on the part of these people; their improvidence, their wickedness; is, by Heavens! enough to—Now look at that couple, will you!"
>
> Well? They were worth looking at. And marriage seemed as reasonable and fair a deed as they need have in contemplation.
>
> "A man may live to be as old as Methuselah," said Mr. Filer, "and may labour all his life for the benefit of people such as those; and may heap up facts on figures, facts on figures, facts on figures, mountains high and dry; and he can no more hope to persuade 'em that they have no right or business to be married, than he can hope to persuade 'em that they have no earthly right or business to be born. And *that* we know they haven't. We reduced it to a mathematical certainty long ago!"[13]

Alderman Cute adds, in his capacity as a local magistrate, that he intends to "Put Down" anyone troubled or in need as a consequence of any ill-advised marriage—and he makes dire predictions about Meg's marriage: a breach with her husband and her fall into economic distress; her bad, shoeless sons running wild in the streets; her husband dying young and leaving her a homeless and sick mother who hangs or drowns herself. The couple listen and walk away, crushed, their affection chilled, Meg weeping.

Toby has also doubted the prudence of Meg's marriage to Richard and—arrogantly warned in his turn by Alderman Cute—does not protest against their broken engagement, for which attitude he is punished. In the course of the night, church bells, whose portentous sounds pour around the daily struggles of his life, summon him to the top of their tower, from which he falls to his death—or so he is made to believe. Seemingly revived as a ghost, Toby witnesses the future deadly consequences of the couple's failure to marry young, much as Ebenezer Scrooge with his ghostly guides witnesses the future deadly consequences of his hard-heartedness. Toby sees Richard going to visit Meg in the poor room where she, worn and prematurely aged, toils at her piecework embroidery for a wretched sub-subsistence. Richard too, has been devastated: "A slouching, moody, drunken sloven, wasted by intemperance and vice, and with his matted hair and unshorn beard in wild disorder; but with some traces on him, too, of having been a man of good proportion and good features in his youth."[14]

He brings news, and a purse full of money, from Lilian, a protégée and companion of Meg. This is Dickens, so I need to backtrack over the usual convoluted plot. On that fateful night of the broken engagement, after the encounter with the repressive gentlemen, Toby delivers a message for one of them and, on his way home, literally runs into the displaced, hunted peasant Will Fern, who is carrying his little orphaned niece Lilian in his arms as he hikes toward refuge in the city with an old acquaintance. Since the very message Toby just took was in aid of persecuting Will, he warns Will and gives him and Lilian refuge in his own poor quarters, and Meg and Lilian bond instantly. Now, years after Meg and Richard's breakup and Toby's death, when the two women have worn themselves out striving alone together for an honest living, Lilian has given up and become a prostitute. It is her tainted money that Richard brings to Meg as the unseen spirit of Toby watches. Meg refuses it with horror, and Richard leaves. Lilian arrives later, falls on her knees before Meg in rapturous repentance, and expires. Some while after this, Richard, who has sunk lower and lower over the years through his wretched bachelorhood, is told by a last-chance prospective employer that only marriage to Meg can save him. He throws himself on her mercy, and they marry, but it is too late. He falls back into his bad habits and then becomes deathly ill. Overextended between taking care of him and her baby, Meg loses her piecework job. After Richard's death, the ruined, despairing Will—another victim of Richard and Meg's failure to marry and, together with Toby, provide a secure home—visits Meg with bodings of suicidal and incendiary rebellion. Meg walks the inclement streets in a vain search for sustenance, and on returning to the room for which she is unable to pay rent, she is barred from entering. To her unseen, hovering father's horror, Meg trudges to the river to drown herself along with her infant daughter.

But lo, it was all a dream. In reality, Toby lives, and after the bells chime at midnight, he discovers to his ecstasy that on this very next day, New Year's Day, Richard and Meg are to be married. The good people of the neighborhood turn up already with music, food, and dancing to celebrate the union. All will now be well.

This fable turns Victorian social and economic reality on its head. The historical counterparts of Meg and Richard, like present-day teenagers in love and determined to marry right away, could have had a decent chance of staying together and prospering only if they waited. How would the couple manage if, in the *best* Dickensian scenario, they marry young, both survive, and have many children? Where would the real, historical Toby and his household be if his wife had lived to have seven or eight more babies after Meg? The messenger cannot fend off hunger or afford rent as it is, even with his daughter working too. As for Meg and Richard, they have been able to save nothing; they do not have the money for a community celebration, the traditional means test for a couple looking to set up a home. Their party is provided spontaneously by neighbors, as if this ever happens in reality. Imagine organizing a feast and dance for neighbors' children when they impulsively decide overnight to wed.

The couple might have for their use, among Toby's poor things, the proverbial pot to piss in, but they do not have the proverbial window to throw the contents out of. Their home will presumably be the converted stable or mews in which Toby and Meg live, and in which they are sheltering Will and Lilian too. One more baby a year could be sharing this small, makeshift dwelling, sleeping on rags and straw and gnawed on by disease-carrying vermin. Medical care, warm clothes, nourishing food, schools and apprenticeships—all these things were out of reach for the numerous children of poor parents, parents who married young and impetuously because they were in love or just because other sexual outlets were forbidden. But there was plenty of work in mines and factories for the children from an early age.

Dickens cultivated a reputation for tenderheartedness, supporting charitable institutions that helped women and children in distress and swooping down as a rescuer in individual tragic cases that came to his attention. His politics were fairly progressive for his time; he supported, for example, better opportunities for women to make an adequate living. But he had the greatest power and influence by far as a writer, and in that capacity, he wielded a deadly sentimentality about existential matters for the underclass and blasted as coldhearted hypocrites those who applied their brains and their informed sympathies to the conditions that made or broke poor families: economists like Filer in "The Chimes," social reformers like Alderman Cute, and moralists like Ebenezer Scrooge—people who had harsh but realistic opinions about what made life worse for the poor. Early, imprudent marriage was near the top of every sane list, whereas Dickens virtually insisted that it was a cure-all for those living on the edge.

In this, he was in effect catering to a cynical and dehumanizing economic shortcut that was manifesting during his time. The big challenge for modern civilization is not that younger males—Richard stands for them in "The Chimes"—must, urgently and early, be tamed by marriage and family responsibility. In such a civilization, there are in fact many ways to socialize male youth: parents' dedicated attention, schooling, apprenticeships, good entry-level jobs, military officer training, all kinds of supervised sports and recreations. The problem is that this socialization is troublesome and expensive. All those arrangements devoted to building character take untold time, energy, and material goods away from more swiftly and crudely productive activities.

The eighteenth- and nineteenth-century Anglican vicarage, for example, where a father worked from home and presided from his study, spun off an untold number of sons as learned professionals and entrepreneurs, scientists and inventors and explorers, artists and writers. But to concentrate the resources for that much cultivation, a large cut of revenue from the parish went to the support of the vicar's household. The resource-intensive model of the Reverend Dodgson, Lewis Carroll's father, for keeping his boys out of trouble and on the road to becoming fathers like himself was obviously not what the Victorian apostles of mass production had in mind for children situated several classes below their own. They needed something cheap and easy, something semiautomatic, to tame poor males. Well, nobody was cheaper or more biddable than marriageable girls; thousands already poured out housework and care for family members for no pay at all, hid their limitations, and shorted their own well-being and opportunities for the sake of others. If young married men became only domesticated enough to be steady wage-earners, then so much the better; this was a crude transformation that a young fertile wife could effect for free, and as a bonus, she would be producing a new generation of cheap labor.

The notion of the young woman as a civilizer through marriage is rife in Victorian popular literature, including novels by William Makepeace Thackeray, Wilkie Collins, George Eliot, Anthony Trollope, and George Meredith. But other novelists never assert that this is the right way to go if a young couple will have virtually nothing—no help to speak of from their parents' generation (which is on the edge itself), no home of their own, no steady modest income.

But Dickens in "The Chimes" went so far as to insist that such a couple should throw itself into the arms of fate at the behest of a dreamlike numinous authority, without even an unconvincing assurance that things will somehow work out for them. Instead, they should be fully and cheerfully willing to suffer without end if need be, since the "advancement" and "improvement" their marriage will purportedly serve might make life better only in a future that no longer includes them. When Toby is supernaturally summoned to the church's bell tower to undergo the crucial revelation, the spirits of the chimes he finds there are fierce, swarming, protean, rather monstrous creatures, who do not hold out any promise that if Meg and Richard do the right thing in marrying immediately, and if Toby does the right thing in approving and rejoicing, everyone concerned will enjoy a happy ending. The only assured outcome is that the correct choices will serve a mysterious authority that might easily be confused with that of Victorian industrial capitalism promising a pie in the sky someday in return for the sacrifices of the poor on the altar of the rich—including sacrifices in the form of their many children.

> "The voice of Time," said the Phantom, "cries to man, Advance! Time is for his advancement and improvement; for his greater worth, his greater happiness, his better life; his progress onward to that goal within its knowledge and its view, and set there, in the period when Time and He [God?] began. Ages of darkness, wickedness, and violence, have come and gone—millions uncountable, have suffered, lived, and died—to point the way before him. Who seeks to turn him back, or stay him on his course, arrests a mighty engine which will strike the meddler dead; and be the fiercer and the wilder, ever, for its momentary check!"[15]

Toby protests that he never offered any such resistance, to his knowledge. He gets the thunderous reply that he is among those who have wronged the chimes by confusing their message with "disregard, or stern regard, of any hope, or joy, or pain, or sorrow, of the many-sorrowed throng" or "any creed that gauges human passions and affections, as it gauges the amount of miserable food on which humanity may pine and wither." In other words, a couple's desire to be bonded together is not to be violated by any material calculation. That calculation appears to be the one crime in the world that the chimes choose to prosecute.[16]

The bells convey that the crime has manifested in closely related ways: Toby stands accused of calculating on his own whether an early marriage can be materially sustained, and he is accused of listening to the "Putters Down of crushed and broken natures"—the busybodies who look ahead and try to make sure that the economy is survivable for everyone, and in particular, that couples do not marry and have children in situations that bode disaster. And so Toby has turned his back upon the "fallen." His punishment begins with hearing terrifying cries of mourning and seeing his own body dead at the foot of the tower, as if he has already fallen and died. He continues to be tormented with harrowing visions, including of his daughter's ruin and death due to delayed marriage and the related destruction of all those closest to her. The forgiveness he now pleads for will be reified in his daughter's joyful wedding the next day.

But he, not she, is the one on the spot to ensure that the right thing happens. Quite emphatically in Dickens, a fertile woman has no proper role in thinking about the future and acting on what she thinks. If Toby must be brought very harshly into line and made to serve the mighty, inscrutable machine the bells extol, the demands on Meg are even harsher. She must produce from her own body the utopian, maximalist future the chimes portend, and she is in no way consulted. She has no chance to question whether such a future is really coming, and, if so, whether her required contribution to it is fair. In a chilling sense, she *is* the engine the chimes insist must grindingly labor on and on, producing new life without a pause and making short work of any considerations that stand in the way of this.

SO WHY IS "THE CHIMES," AN ALARMINGLY RADICAL TALE but such an obscure one that it could not in itself have had much influence, my basis for writing about Dickens's attitude toward fertility? The novella would be easy to brush off if it represented only a phase in the author's thinking, a passing mood, a distortion of his otherwise benign or practical ideology concerning the family. Many writers' viewpoints on such a sensitive matter change over time, under pressure from their own life cycles, or through their exposure to other ways of thinking and living. Tolstoy developed from the priapic young husband who subjected his wife to many wearing pregnancies to a strong proponent of celibacy who regarded his ongoing desire for his wife as a spiritually ruinous temptation, and the existence of all his children but his favorite daughter as an irritating distraction from his utopian projects.

But Dickens was remarkably consistent over his entire career. He had a weird belief in the power of children to repair and elevate dismal situations, as opposed to a rational recognition that children are more or less helpless and in urgent need of care and guidance themselves, and that only exploiters, abusers, and hypocrites feel otherwise. "The Chimes" is, granted, an unusually cruel and thoughtless expression of Dickens's worldview. The story insists, basically, that Toby commits a mortal sin in rationally worrying that his daughter and her sweetheart, if they marry, will not be able to support their children. But this message is in synch with the main theme of Dickens's fictional works: Providence will, in one way or another, come to the rescue of every deserving child, no matter how chancy, miserable, or desperate the circumstances into which that child is born.

Dickens's functionally very broad definition of what providence is can give this theme rather horrifying implications as it plays out in some stories. Providence is not, as usual in fiction, the force that provides for the protagonist's future; providence is whatever provides a satisfying thrill to others—readers or the fictional characters who are onlookers—including the thrill of tender pity or righteous anger at a child's demise. Hence Dickensian narrative orchestration may leave the onlookers very happy with the death of a virtuous waif, such as Smike in *Nicholas Nickleby* or Little Nell in *The Old Curiosity Shop*, a waif who has gone through many poignant sacrifices, harrowing dangers, and bizarre persecutions (originally, these events were revealed over the many months it took for a novel to appear, episode by episode, in a magazine). After all that, a nice deathbed scene is a big relief, and a good cry just the thing.

Throughout the ages, natural checks on some couples' fertility have been moral and emotional, along the lines of "How could we stand to see our child hungry, or ragged, or scorned by better-off children?" and "A daughter we had wouldn't have a dowry, and a son wouldn't have an education." Dickens turns such considerations on their head by insisting that the child born in dire straits is the *source* of all that is best in life: delight, love, good fortune, justice, inspiration, even material support, care, and nurturance. The orphaned Little Nell endures an odyssey of perils and hardships to care for and protect her grandfather when they are both homeless. Amy Dorrit, who gives her name to the novel *Little Dorrit*, is the youngest child of a man long imprisoned for debt; she was born in the prison and now slaves at sewing to support her father and even hides their circumstances from outsiders in order to save his pride.

But, again, Dickens maneuvers away from the depiction of meaningless, comprehensively appalling exploitation and sacrifice of children and youths. Many of the young protagonists emerge from seeming dead ends of hardship through Dickens's rescue fantasies, for which he no doubt nurtured a propensity while monotonously toiling in a factory as a little boy. Nicholas Nickleby, a half-orphan thrown out onto the world's mercies by his cruel uncle, has only to tell his story of serial woes to the solid businessman Charles Cheeryble to be believed, and in short order provided with a well-paying job, a house to live in with his sister and mother, and help in vindicating his wrongs. And Nicholas is a savior in his own right. His confederate Smike was born a risk to his father's position in society, hidden away, then abandoned to menial work and abuse. But he finds transcendent comfort and meaning in the care Nicholas gives him during his mortal illness, and he perishes in the bliss of mutual love. Oliver Twist is the illegitimate son of a woman who dies giving birth to him, and he falls through a laughable social safety net into a gang of pickpockets, but this does not prevent him from meeting up with just the right saviors at just the right moments, and he finds surviving family members, secures his inheritance, and is ensconced in a wealthy, loving home. Perhaps the most heartrending orphan in Dickens's oeuvre is Little Nell. Her tireless charm and goodness secure her crucial refuges, including the one in which she dies; she was so impressive to readers that some of them provided her with a real gravesite.

We are unthinkingly used to this paradigm of never-failing ragamuffin appeal and transcendence, as if it were the old wallpaper in a lifelong home, but it was a major shake-up to the culture when it first appeared. True, an immemorial basic of Western storytelling is the special child who is imperiled or just whisked into obscurity at a very young age, who is providentially protected (usually by people other than his parents), and who later comes into his own: Moses, Oedipus, a small army of the half-mortal sons of gods and goddesses, Jesus, Arthur, Tom Jones, and many others. But these figures are *born* special, and they are destined for greatness because it is their birthright. In Dickens, the drama of providence for children is extended to all classes and a bewildering variety of situations, and oddly it includes protagonists who do not survive to triumph or even reach adulthood but perish prematurely and most pitifully. The old lesson is that the path to leadership can be hard, but that the correct bloodline will win out; the new, Dickensian one is that a childhood cannot go horribly *and* meaninglessly wrong, even for the reason that the child never had a calculable chance. Before Dickens, Western culture was crammed with fantasy about the children of the elite, and about the gifted and lucky who might start in some low station (witness Grimms' fairy tales, and the tailor who can slay giants and marry a princess); but it went without saying that those born to suffer in the shadows suffered in the shadows.[17] Dickens planted, rooted, and grew the paradox that such children were the darlings of destiny. If they did not prosper, they would die in poignant glory.

Dickens's magic-waif formula has had a pervasive and profound influence on modern ideas about family formation. He was the first of the modern mega-celebrity authors, and still holds the world record for the most sales of an individual book, *A Tale of Two Cities*, at more than 200,000,000 copies. His novels and novellas have been translated into nearly every language in which books are published.[18] The currency of religious texts (the Bible leading the way), each as a sum of various translations and editions of original texts, has of course been greater, but Dickens's novels have in some ways rivaled scripture through their ritualistic uses. The tales, most of which were originally serialized, were read out loud episode by episode to Victorian families keen for the next plot twist, and actually proved tough competition for customary prayers and pious readings directed at the gathered household. The appeal of Dickens has of course diminished, but to this day, the *Christmas Carol* story in one form or another regularly features in Yuletide entertainment.

Aside from his enormous and enthralled readership, Dickens drew great crowds as a speaker. He and Abraham Lincoln were prototypes of the charismatic orator with previously undreamed-of reach in an age when both the orator and the listeners could travel much greater distances to come together. But Dickens's reach as a public speaker was international, and his role as a philanthropist gave him great credibility when he asked people to change their hearts and lives on his say-so.

And change them they did. Dickens crept into the West's collective bones and imparted, as the Bible does, commanding notions of what is natural, virtuous, and worthwhile. Long after Queen Victoria's holiday family tableaux fell into obscurity, Dickensian imagery and sentiments ruled. There should be many children around the evening fireplace and the holiday table. A little girl's tender gaze will melt any amount of adult woe, so it does not really matter that she is growing up in dire or squalid conditions; she is, like Meg with her marvelous comforting, unassertive eyes, an automated woe-melter, not a whole human being with her own imperative needs. If children have spilled over to a life on the street, they are raffishly adorable and wiser about what really matters than churlish, pedantic adults. Such children are readily rescuable through spontaneous goodwill, and tenderness toward them will undo any damage they have suffered.[19]

Dickens's words have also been the underpinning for common practices and institutions, especially in the English-speaking world, where his status has been outright magisterial. Witness, for instance, the huge American popularity of stranger adoption, and the commitment to make that bond the same as the one between parents and their biological children. The Bible has nothing to do with this; the infertility dramas there—of Sarah, of Rachel, of Hannah, of Elizabeth—would be meaningless if children had been thought able to fall perfectly into place in strange homes through the operations of the divine will; that is, if children were interchangeable. In the Bible, it is only important births to important parents that God decrees and brings about.

Dickens's influence on the willingness to adopt is arguably benign on balance; he probably did more than any other single person to empty orphanages and to open capable homes to children of parents who could not cope with them or just did not want them. But Dickens also originated and diffused a cultlike and destructive tenet: Children need to be born even in the most unpromising circumstances since we can assume everything will turn out hunky-dory. "Hunky-dory" is *very* broadly defined and doesn't necessarily include the children's welfare or even their survival. Children's suffering is supposed to be an edifying drama, and their deaths inspiring.

This is the tenet the antiabortion movement has absorbed, and the one that it expresses in asserting that somewhere there is a loving family for any seemingly hopeless baby—and even if not, every rationally hopeless pregnancy must still come to term: The Christian God has (like the animated church bells in "The Chimes") a relentless will to evoke life and use it for ineffable and unquestionable purposes. In his fictional works, Dickens greases the agonies and deaths of children lacking capable and responsible adults in their lives with a numinous sentimentality in order to cram these outcomes into his pro-fertility schema. In the antiabortion movement, the hideous fallout from blocking reproductive choice—severely disabled children languishing for want of families willing to adopt them, for example, and prisons and mental institutions crowded with people raised by mothers who did not want them—is whitewashed with piety: This is all God's plan to test our acceptance of His will, which is Life at any cost.

But the antiabortion movement is of course much more ambitious than Dickens. He expressed his radical ideas about the family through fiction but made social interventions through ordinary philanthropy, which just sought to care for pregnant women, mothers, and children who were already there. Given that he could pursue his preference for fertility in his own life, he wasn't overly agitated by what other real people did or didn't do. In this, a great author's narcissism was to his credit. He saw himself in both the fictional waifs and the fictional rescuers, and let it go at that. His ideological heirs are not nearly so restrained. For them, the marvelous narrative is a script, and the rest of us a troupe of actors who must be locked in and forced to stage it.

CHAPTER 6

THIS LOOKS ODDLY FAMILIAR

Eugenics and the Holy Image

CHARLES DARWIN (1809–1882) WAS A CONTEMPOrary of Dickens who probably best represents the cerebral, scientific side of Victorian culture. He had, in fact, one of the most remarkable minds in the history of our species. By applying careful logic to tireless observation, he developed an accurate unified theory of life on earth without knowing how the chemistry of biological heredity worked; the double-helix DNA molecule was not mapped until the 1950s.

Perhaps as remarkable as Darwin's intelligence, curiosity, and persistence was his character writ large. Unlike nearly all other intellectuals, he did not frivolously indulge the capacity that some English Bibles translate as "the imagination of the heart." His thought system did not serve his own power and self-justification. It was not untainted by his inherited prejudices—for example, he believed the white race was organically superior—but he never went off into the wild blue yonder of political tangents. For example, though he was concerned that vaccination would degrade specimens generation by generation—farm animals as well as members of our own species—by allowing the less strong to survive and breed, he humanely and commonsensically deplored the "overwhelming present evil" that would come with "intentionally . . . neglect[ing] the weak and helpless."[1] As shown by his dedication as a family man, he could think and feel at the same time, and the idea that we could let nature simply take its course among our fellow human beings alarmed him.

But others were inspired by his theory of evolution to take a sharply contrasting position, called Social Darwinism. They held that superior and inferior natural fitness, not arbitrary hierarchy, was largely responsible for the skewed distribution of power and wealth among humankind. Social Darwinists like Herbert Spencer, William Graham Sumner, and Madison Grant claimed to have drawn a sort of unified theory of economics, sociology, and political science from Darwin's work, and this theory magically padded their own already comfortable perches. Spencer was an editor of *The Economist*, which still today champions a laissez-faire, minimally regulated commercial system as the best sorter and rewarder of ability. Sumner was a Yale professor, a small-government conservative, and opposed to labor unions, opinions that made him popular with business interests during the Gilded Age. Grant was wealthy and extremely well connected, as witnessed by his prominent role in the establishment of the US national parks system.

Leading Social Darwinists held that they possessed so many of the good things in life in accordance with the laws of nature, much as they had inherited their eye color, their eagle gaze, and their impressive facial hair. Intellectual slobs of the usual patriarchal kind, they did not hesitate over the reality of other people's thoughts (and suffering, aspirations, attachments, and lives) but instead produced nasty propaganda. Grant's *The Passing of the Great Race: Or, The Racial Basis of European History* (1916) warned of the demise of the United States if the Northern European or "Nordic" race there did not retain high numbers relative to other races.

Grant had adopted the refinement of Social Darwinism called "eugenics" (the pseudoscience that favored the "well-born"). Eugenicists stressed the threatening forces of alleged biological inferiority, and so wanted radical change, not just affirmation and shoring up of existing power. Eugenicists claimed to be so alarmed that the underclasses, the unhealthy, and the wrong races were going to outbreed and interbreed with the right ones that they advocated state intervention and were successful in curtailing immigration from Southern Europe and in instituting forced sterilization of the sick, the disabled, sometimes people who were merely dark or poor, and women and girls given labels such as "morally insane" because they had had sex outside marriage.[2]

The early twentieth century was the carefree heyday of eugenics, before the Nazi embrace of these ideas showed their potential to inspire large-scale atrocity. The playing out of "scientific" racism on battlefields and conquered territories, in concentration camps, and in forced labor installations was a culminating demonstration of the evil a state causes in trying to classify and commandeer human biological diversity for its own purposes.

But the story I have to tell about eugenics concerns the special role that one woman thought leader played in the movement. The eugenics campaign addressing women in particular could from its start be insinuatingly intimate because women authors fostered it. In the new information culture, an older and more experienced female relative or neighbor or a nurse or midwife from the neighborhood no longer gave the critical or exclusive advice. It was someone in the media, distant and untouchable in her authority but claiming to be trustworthy due to her better knowledge of the shared female condition. Moreover, misty fantasies of maternal bliss, and aspirational imagery of upper-class ease and prestige figured largely in the work of one of these leaders. In these ways, eugenic messages wormed their way into the culture and are still very much with us, their poisonous potential unsuspected.

By the early twentieth century women had become far more vocal and visible in the professions, as reformers (especially through the slavery abolition and temperance movements) and most especially as agitators for the right to vote. Though they lacked the social freedom, access to institutions, and power in the economy that men enjoyed, some women substantially made up for their restrictions through writing and publishing. A young woman could prepare for a brilliant career as an author in the privacy of her home and in whatever leisure time she was allowed, as Virginia Woolf did; feminism is, in fact, strongly associated with female authorship, most classically in the case of Virginia Woolf's essay "A Room of One's Own," about women's relative ability to study, think, and write independently. Naturally, women were going to cover a topic of great interest to other women, which was access to the safe, effective family planning methods that began to appear in the nineteenth century: the diaphragm, the cervical cap, improved condoms made from the latex of rubber trees, and female surgical sterilization.

But the eugenics movement, which plainly sprung from the male urge to control women and families from the top of society, coopted and tainted much of women's advocacy in this realm. This seems in general to have happened because advocates saw eugenics as the only power game in town for furthering their practical interests around childbearing, rather than because they were convinced ideologues themselves, with a sincere commitment to genetic warfare of any kind. In the US, the most influential female voice for "birth control" (her coinage) was Margaret Sanger (1879–1966), whose origins were working-class Irish, and whose mother had died at the age of fifty after the birth of eleven children and seven lost pregnancies. Sanger developed her concern for women's health further while working as a visiting nurse in slums, where she identified large families as a basic source of misery; the women there pined for the means they assumed their well-to-do contemporaries had for keeping their pregnancies few.

Sanger was raised with socialist ideals, and it looks very unlikely that she was ever spurred by racial—much less class—hatred. But through miracles of tact and pragmatism, she strove in the cause of family limitation even in cooperation with the Ku Klux Klan. Nevertheless, on her worst day she was a heroic champion of family planning who did not let prosecutions and time in jail deter her. She spread factual information, popularized new methods, founded woman-friendly clinics, and lobbied and organized politically. Her American Birth Control League became

Planned Parenthood. The year before her death, the about-face in popular consensus that might have taken much longer without her was ratified in 1965 when the Supreme Court's *Griswold v. Connecticut* ruling legalized contraception for married couples over the whole of the United States.

The most important British advocate for family limitation was Marie Stopes (1880–1958). Her career was superficially similar to that of Sanger's, her sometime collaborator. But Stopes was not the rock on which reproductive rights and access were built in Britain. Her clinics did not prosper over time, and the nonprofit organization named after her, Marie Stopes International, eventually came to be known as MSI Reproductive Choices.

The awkwardness of using her name explicitly has obvious causes. MSI delivers reproductive health services in the developing world, as far as possible without regard to ideology or culture. The principle is that girls and women know best what is good for themselves, and so they should choose for themselves.[3] Marie Stopes would be a poor figurehead for any campaign to realize this present consensus of liberals, progressives, and moderates because she was a convinced and passionate eugenicist.

She was keenly interested only in the thriving of the middle and upper-middle classes, and she did not trust even these people to thrive by their own lights, with the mere instrumental help of more information and better technology. Instead, she published over the years a spiritual and moral program, a serial script she held to be key for the elevation of "the race"—pure-blooded white Northern Europeans.[4] The poor, who were most in need of her aid and compassion, she viewed mainly as breeders of criminals, misfits, and public charges, whose fertility should be curtailed, by law if necessary. Because she was so plainly disinclined to meet the less fortunate where they were, her eventual attempts at course correction were of little use to her personally. The kind of clinical resources for which she helped advocate found increasing acceptance, while she herself met with increasing scorn and skepticism.

THE MODERN WEST'S HISTORY OF EFFORTS TO RECKON with the deeper and wider meanings of reproductive biology—including Jean-Baptiste Lamarck's theory that traits acquired during an animal's life can be passed down to its offspring, Thomas Malthus's mathematical panic that human breeding would surpass the human food supply, and of course the over-stimulating accuracies of Darwin—is a mammoth and hypercomplex subject. But even I (a Classicist by training) can see the outsized role of Western intellectualizing in action here. In other cultures, the powerful are inclined to *demonstrate* what they think about fertility: by laws and material incentives and by the ad hoc treatment of subjugated women (that is, most or all women).

But for Westerners, much of the control has been enacted through talking and writing, through heavy-handed and manipulative persuasion. In the realm of fertility particularly, the worst brutalities—the witch hunts, the forced sterilizations in America under eugenics laws, an array of Nazi atrocities in pursuit of the Nordic "Master Race's" dominance—were ushered in by propaganda that convinced people to cooperate. The scale of the damage done by the West in the name of its ideologies (imperialism, mercantilism, racism, colonialism, communism, fascism, capitalism) isn't unrelated to the ultimate misuse of that biblical "imagination of the heart," a misuse that Darwin so staunchly resisted:

the grand, powerful, abstract vision that makes us believe we can transform the world merely by sitting on our duffs and broadcasting out that vision.

This is why I am going to look at eugenics not through social or medical or legal or economic history, and only incidentally in relation to the big events such as mass migrations and world wars—though eugenics is certainly linked to all of these—but through a milestone in its literature, Marie Stopes's *Radiant Motherhood*, published in 1920. In this book she not only gives advice, including on family limitation, for married happiness and stability—that advice began with *Married Love* and *Wise Parenthood: A Treatise on Birth Control or Contraception*, both published in 1918—but lays out a fuller program for motherhood.

The sweeping yet nitpicking, dreamy yet hectoring manner of *Radiant Motherhood* does not represent a mere sideshow to an otherwise sober and fact-grounded career as an author, though in a parallel professional life Stopes was an accomplished evolutionary botanist with publications aimed at her scientific peers. Her projections of herself to the public at large are very different, and include volumes of romantic, erotic, mystical, and exotic poetry and drama. In her personal life, she was not the sort to shrink from ending her first marriage with a public scandal by seeking a divorce on the grounds of her husband's impotence, and she had a passionate relationship with a married man who was Japanese—an extremely daring move for a British woman of her time. Her writing even on maternal health and nutrition reflects her distinct, exhibitionist sensuality, which is evidenced in certain photos of her: provocative stare, come-hither poses, diaphanous drapery, visible nipples.[5] She had showy run-ins with the Anglican church and other advocates of traditional morality when she insisted on eroticism as the great guiding and elevating force in the universe.

In a crowning irony, considering her main mission in life as an advisor to mothers and potential mothers, she does not come across as strongly maternal herself, or even as a particularly good mother. She did not give birth until she was thirty-nine. The first child was stillborn. A later child survived, and she had a creepy, clingy, hypercontrolling relationship with him. Using him as a foil, she quite brutally vetted several children she took into her home with a view to adoption. She doesn't seem to have been above, for example, terrorizing a little boy into bed-wetting and then berating him for his "filthy" transgression.

But she did have a knack for projecting extensive and objective knowledge about sex, pregnancy, childbirth, and early motherhood. Another category of her photos shows her soberly dressed, serious-faced, and doing her professional work as a scientist—but her university position had nothing to do with human health or behavior. In her eugenics activism, she speaks as if with the authority of a clinician or a health or social researcher, not an amateur who relied for many of her impressions on letters she received from women.

She did, however, have a keen instinct for uniting the personality, experience, and capacities she did have to create the impression of a complete and compelling world like that of the novelist Dickens, only purporting to be real. Perhaps most powerful was her combination of the age-old drama of the ingenue, on her perilous way to marriage and motherhood, with the new law of the cultural jungle, that sex sells. Film, print fiction, advertisements, the fashion industry, and the music hall now retailed the body with an exuberance and lack of apology that hadn't been the norm since the ancient world. Add to this the ever-burgeoning prestige and solemnity of science—a cornucopia of discoveries and practically applicable technical advances spanning recent centuries (with everything from the germ theory of disease to the steam engine) and culminating in the ability to fly—and you had a heady mixture.

From a personal viewpoint, childbearing might have been surprising subject matter for Stopes to latch onto, but for an ambitious pundit, it was a brilliant choice. There was a particularly great need for an informational linkup between sex and fertility. Victorian ignorance and fear of the body and its desires reigned into the Edwardian era and beyond, and people urgently wanted more freedom, relationships that served their individual needs better, and more control over the direction of their lives than their parents had had. More control over the results of sex was essential to pursuing these aspirations.

But up to now the authoritative published guides for those beginning their sex lives were aimed mainly at persuading boys not to masturbate and girls and young women to refrain, conform, and do their duty all around. In these latter volumes, devoted mainly to cleanliness, etiquette, menstruation management, and healthful diet and exercise, readers might well have grown irritated searching for what exactly it was that they were not supposed to do until they were married, so you have to wonder how they could have reliably avoided doing it.[6] Even straightforward information about the mechanics of sex and venereal disease was widely considered polluting and corrupting. I'm reminded of Lady Bracknell's dictum in *The Importance of Being Earnest*: "Ignorance is like a delicate, exotic fruit; touch it, and the bloom is gone." These volumes tended to play on dreams and ideals of romantic love and domestic bliss, and might even reference novels and fairy tales, but their heavy-handedness was fairly plain and crude.

Within the framework of eugenics—which was the most authoritative template of the time for thinking about fertility—Stopes came up with a form of advice book that addressed these deficits in quite a titillating and appealing manner. And she struck publishing and punditry gold. Her first such book, *Married Love* (1918), sold two thousand copies in its first two weeks, a startling rate for that era. *Married Love* was legally sold in America only starting in 1931, after a ban to protect public morals that made the title a sensation. Some of Margaret Sanger's books—notably *Women and the New Race* (1920) and *The Pivot of Civilization* (1922)—also caused great excitement and sold robustly.

But Sanger had no special calling as a writer; she was a nurse and activist who saw writing as one means to ameliorate the suffering she deplored. Stopes was a *born* writer, and she readily set about infusing her personal dream of marriage and motherhood onto the page and into her readers. In this dream, young Anglo-Saxon women of means were not just suffering less as they reached their greater potential as mothers. They were called to the center of a vivid panorama of perfection, a heaven of sex and motherhood, as a reward for unflagging eugenic faith and good works, with a vista to the whole race's transcendence. For this fulfillment, the ethereally pure character and healthy and ravishing person of the heroine and the gentlemanly delicacy and unfailing devotion of the hero must overcome all obstacles and bring them the perfect heir, which is the most precious gift they can make in turn to their race's future.

This was, however, not an uplifting, idealizing, and fantasizing novel or folktale; it was supposed to be the story of every couple entitled to reproduce at all. Health, happiness, belonging, and usefulness were not to be found in different individuals' different adjustments. No, everything had to happen according to Stopes's soaring creative vision. In *Radiant Motherhood* (1920), she insists that a woman must glow like enriched uranium, and that this alone generates the kind of children that "the Race" needs for its rather vague but certainly ethereal destiny, some kind of melding of beauty, spirituality, and power. To start with:

> Every lover desires a child. Those who imagine the contrary, and maintain that love is purely selfish, know only of the lesser types of love. The supreme love of true mates always carries with it the yearning to perpetuate the exquisite quality of its own being, and to record, through the glory of its mutual creation, other lives yet more beautiful and perfect. . . .
>
> Whether early in the days of their marriage or postponed for some months or more out of regard for his wife's body and beauty, the hour will come when the young husband yearning above her, sees in his wife's eyes the reflection of the future, and when their mutual longing springs up to initiate the chain of lives which shall repeat throughout the ages the bodily, mental and spiritual beauties of each other, which each holds so dear. Perhaps in lovers' talk and exquisite whispers they have spoken of this great deed on which they are embarking, and each has voiced that intense yearning which filled them to see another "with your eyes, your hair, your smile," living and radiant. The lovers dream that they will be repeated in others of their own creation, always

young, running through the ages which culminate in the golden glories of the millennium.[7]

"Exquisite," "perfect," "beauty," and "intense," as well as "radiant," are favorite words of Stopes: Reproduction should be fantasy come to life under her close guidance. According to her, things may go wrong in sex, pregnancy, childbirth, and infancy—she improbably makes out that she knows all the hazards—but if these things are more than ripples in the shining stream, then some sin against wholesomeness or joy, or an unfitness to breed in the first place, is likely the cause. Nausea, for example, is not supposed to exist in the ideal, highly qualified pregnant woman she depicts: lovely, sensitive, refined, intelligent but not ambitious, healthy, adored, revered, living carefree in some peaceful and verdant place. In all but the "exceptional and pre-disposed," following a few tips "will ensure complete freedom from morning sickness." Among these tips, Stopes directs that "garments of the lightest wool or silk if possible ... should be so lightly hung that a butterfly can walk the length of her body without tearing its wings."[8]

But a titanium fist is inside the gossamer authorial glove. Stopes holds that tender, aesthetic, or conscientious feeling itself can and must be supervised and controlled, managed for the proper results, just as health and the inheritance of biological fitness must be.

> I know, for instance, one man who fainted at the time his wife gave birth to their child, and who, under no consideration, would allow her to have a second child, although he had intensely desired and looked forward to the fatherhood of a large family before he knew the actual physical expe-

riences which it entailed. Such a man, in my opinion, was a good father wasted by an excess of emotion made all the more intensely destructive to himself by the endeavour to maintain the totally artificial and indeed the crude attitude which is supposed to be "correct" for a man, namely a sort of dissociation of himself from his wife's experiences and a hardened lack of recognition of all that is involved....

If we are ever to raise our race to the point where every child is so precious that no child can be hungry, neglected or unwanted, the conscious price which the *father* pays for his children will be one of the assets in valuing the children of the nation. It is, therefore, better to acknowledge and encourage such sensitiveness in the father by allowing the open and honourable expression of such feeling, and thus to avoid that almost neurotic and destructive effect of the suppression of such intense feeling as warped the father mentioned above. Because, if the wife avails herself of the advice I give in this book, and if the time for parenthood is chosen rightly and wisely in relation to her general health, and it is ascertained before she embarks upon potential motherhood that her bodily and bony structure is fit for motherhood, then though the experiences of both will be difficult and profound in their testing of the quality of each other, motherhood should not result in excessive strain, and should indeed be a time of wonderful life activity.[9]

The man's feelings, in other words, are instrumental. Since he and his wife are so constituted that they should have a large family, he ought to suffer to that end, and suffer openly the embarrassment of appearing unmanly, so that his sensitive concern is not "wasted" on himself, his wife, and his one child. How many children, by the way, would his wife like to have? Maybe she does not want more either, and her husband's feelings are a convenient excuse in the face of busybodies.

Stopes's is not a psychotherapeutic attitude, holding out the hope that frank and trusting discussion of a life can improve it by building understanding and opening a greater range of choices. This man is not seeking to change, and he does not need to change in order to meet society's essential norms. But what Stopes wants from him is to make the Olympic team in the sport of family formation. He must engender and nurture many strong, beautiful, intelligent, virtuous offspring for the glory of race. And she makes clear that nothing that stands in the way of improving the racial stock can be good or harmless in itself; conversely, no "improvement" is detrimental, or simply impossible, to impose. Whenever a reader might suspect otherwise, she slaps on the labels of condemnation, such as "destructive," "artificial," "neurotic," and "warped." All of these words are applied here to a man who backpedaled when faced with some of the scarier things that happen to women's bodies—hardly an unnatural or necessarily pernicious response, in my view.

But for Stopes, as for a misogynistic Church Father, nothing is "natural" but what, commonsensically, doesn't seem natural at all. And like a member of the Catholic clergy speaking with the authority and power of the church behind him, Stopes had political backing. Proponents of eugenics founded institutes, chaired departments, and published "scientific" journals. They introduced new legislation and made calls in the press for the repression of whole categories of the population, including "paupers." Whenever Stopes inserts among her blandishments an outburst about intolerable blights on the race, she means business.

A book like *Radiant Motherhood* is in fact more sinister in that such outbursts are few; the author concentrates on encouraging, advising, and scolding somewhat like an ordinary good—if overly involved—female friend or relative. But even so, her excesses tally up. She never quits, she never relaxes, she never finds anything she can accept with graceful resignation.

If her expectations of husbands are daunting, then think of the poor wives. No Elizabethan masque, no ballet at the court of Louis the XIV could be more exacting for the performers than the spectacle Stopes has in mind. What she describes is far from just slogging through human reproduction and care of the young in the easiest ways that can be contrived, which is the apparent historical norm. When a woman is sick, exhausted, swollen, experiencing mood-swings, in pain, and undergoing at least some trauma, nothing must be a more obvious recourse than to be surrounded by nonjudgmental care—to feel the altruism and tolerance of a community upholding motherhood when it begins.

Too bad, when it comes to the modern, "scientific" regime of eugenic childbearing. To participate, women must prance prettily in a sort of dog show, a display of breeding stock, while the organizers remain indifferent to the torments attached to such exquisite creatures (the tails docked from puppies, the weird conformations achieved by selective breeding that can make it hard to walk or breathe). Indeed, our treasures have no business minding what they are put through, so important are they, so elevating our use of them must be:

A young woman whose character is sufficiently beautiful and sensitive to know the highest joys of motherhood—the full delights of human existence and love—will also be sensitive to the varied pains that motherhood will bring. . . .

The radiance of the highest form of motherhood is that of the transfigured saint, hallowed by suffering comprehended and endured, transmuted into a service beyond and above the lower desires of self.[10]

In Stopes's mania for "radiance," she puts off on other women a very personal-sounding revulsion at a thickened figure, discolored skin, and breasts with a mature shape; a very personal-sounding terror that, once a young woman's beauty is impaired by pregnancy, the crystal sphere around the lovers will be shattered and the woman will dissolve in self-disgust, her mate reduced to a pathetic puddle beside her. She is supposed to need a lofty spiritual attitude just to be able to cast her eyes on her new shortcomings.

But, again, Stopes writes off most of these harms as temporary, easily remedied, or the result of bad living or a bad attitude; a superior woman, worthy to be a mother, will rise above them by precise adherence to this or that advice—some of which happens to be in reality ignorant, whimsical, and dangerous. Whereas six weeks of limited activity even after an uncomplicated childbirth is restoring and recommended, Stopes decrees that new mothers lounge in luxurious immobility, like odalisques. Most women could not get away with this and wouldn't want to; those who did might develop bedsores, urinary tract infections, deep vein thrombosis, or pneumonia—besides neglecting their babies.

Part of Stopes's bad advice is understandable given the slow progress in gynecological and obstetric science, and in related fields such as nutrition, particularly at the early stages of her career as a motherhood pundit. One thing the British elite did grasp, because of the nation's long history with a navy and a merchant fleet that made prolonged voyages, was the dangers of scurvy to general health and well-being. Lower-middle-class pregnant women might not be able to afford the regular dose of vitamin C found in a lemon or lime that sailors received for free. Stopes was right to recommend orange juice at breakfast and to rail at the high cost of oranges. She was wrong to try to pass off orange juice as a magical elixir, especially when she also warned against a rich, hearty, high-protein diet for pregnant women. Stopes was likely motivated in her decree by old notions of the indelicacy of women eating "men's" foods (chops, steaks, game, bacon and eggs, cheese), and no doubt shuddered at the thought of a sylphlike figure gaining weight.

Stopes certainly wasn't contemplating the whole sweep of what people go through to form their families. She could bear only the thought of success adhering to virtue, failure adhering to inadequacy. She was not seeking, and certainly not passing on, stories of reproductive mediocrity and suggesting the best that could be done in given circumstances. She cherished competitive excellence, such as she herself had achieved—laboriously, against the odds—as an academic scientist. She quotes, for example, a letter from a woman who claims that during her pregnancies she lived "exactly as usual," playing golf until halfway through the seventh month and bicycling until the end, and that she was shopping on the day of the second birth, her condition unguessed-at by the acquaintance who was with her. Another woman claims that her "splendid specimen" came from a fifteen-minute, unattended labor, with no pain.[11]

The performance that Stopes expected of the women she wrote to and for was by no means limited to biological fitness and the mother's behavior during pregnancy. Stopes cautions expectant mothers against being in the wrong mood, thinking the wrong thoughts, having the wrong wishes. She even suspects that homosexual recruitment might be a sort of prenatal mesmerism—perhaps this is an early version of the psychiatric theory that mothers make their sons gay by raising them wrong:

> Oscar Wilde, whose genius was sullied by terrible sex crimes, which he expiated in prison, is known to all the world as a type whose distressing perversion is a racial loss. His mother once confided to an old friend that all the time she was carrying her son Oscar, she was intensely and passionately desiring a daughter, visualizing a girl, and, as far as possible, using all the intensity of purpose which she possessed to have a girl, and that she often in after years blamed herself bitterly, because she felt that possibly his perverted proclivities were due to some influence she might have had upon him while his tiny body was being moulded.[12]

The demand for perfect eugenic behavior extends to forming the minds of young children. For this purpose, there are pages of scripting in *Radiant Motherhood* concerning the facts of life. Here, for example, is the smarmy verbiage that creeps toward informing a child that he first developed in his mother's midsection and therefore owes her love, obedience, and silence on these matters except to herself, Daddy, and God.

"What is being born?"

"Being born is being shown to the world and seeing the world for the first time. At the end of nine months after God and Daddy and Mummy started to make you, you were ready to open your eyes and breathe and cry, and be a real live baby, and that day they showed you to somebody and you saw the world. That was being born."

"Where was I before you finished making me?"

"Mummy kept you hidden away so that nobody at all should see you."

"*Where* was I hidden?"

"You were hidden in a most wonderful place, in the place where only quite little babies can be while God and their mummies are making them."[13]

In these elaborate ways, Stopes plies better-off women, but poor women do not seem to be part of her intended audience, apparently because they should not be thus encouraged to produce their inevitably inferior babies, which threaten to crush civilization with crime, vice, disability, and dependence on the public purse. But this too seems to be expressed emotionally, with weighted imagery; she displays little or no interest in the demography that male eugenicists drew on (or just made a show of drawing on). She is instead preoccupied with lawns, the perfect place for babies to disport themselves, and with the sordid horrors of the city that sicken and debase children raised there.

In one passage of *Radiant Motherhood*, she describes a poorly educated woman who was exasperated when a doctor brushed off her passionate questions and complaints and consigned her to further childbearing with a husband who—as a female medical student recognized—had syphilis, which passed to her babies congenitally and caused them to waste away and die one after the other. In Stopes's story, the woman wants only to stop having babies if there is something "wrong" with her husband; medical treatment, perhaps giving the couple a chance for healthy babies in the future, is not shown as entering her mind. (Syphilis could be treated at the time, though with difficulty, and in a few years penicillin was to make it easily treatable.) It should have entered Stopes's mind but apparently didn't; at any rate, she sounds as if she is projecting onto this poor woman her own fixation on infertility as a solution to social problems and isn't bothered by the thought of the woman left with no children after so many tries, and a lonely and bereft old age.[14] Stopes's imagination, so fervid when it came to the bliss of upper-middle-class childbearing, did not venture into what might make childbearing for the poor something that she would not need to shudder at.

IT MIGHT SEEM SENSIBLE AND DECENT TO WAVE ASIDE ALL of this in Stopes—a difficult personality developed from rare stresses, and political attitudes and associations that she probably would not have clung to early in her career had she known the catastrophic direction in which they were heading—and concentrate on the great good she did in helping bring the issues of maternal and infant health and reproductive choice to the fore. I do favor the dictum that we shouldn't treat great figures in history as if they had had time machines but wickedly refused to use them. I prefer to be grateful for their contributions, however flawed or limited they might have been.

But in this case, more was at play. Marie Stopes encountered struggles and humiliations early in her life, which gave her a mania for control, all the way from stipulating that the right babies (born of ladies in gossamer garments) should crawl on suburban grass and the wrong babies should not exist at all to consigning her husband to live in the attic. Inherited trauma needs a good look and a serious discussion so that it doesn't pass down indefinitely.

That said, for many people dysfunction in the home and in the mind has a big, national background. In addition to personal trauma, Stopes experienced public and historical trauma, the First World War being the most obvious source, after which eugenics soared in popularity and persuasiveness. For almost everyone in Britain the woes of the war were formative (or, rather, destructive), but they would have been a greater shock to a thoughtful, highly educated person like Stopes and to the comfortable and confident classes she chiefly addressed than to those whose comprehensively rough, disregarded lives had given them thick skins and low expectations. In posher, more enlightened circles, the war shook up old habits of leadership and lent itself to fearful speculation about how a future society could recover and hold itself together.

Great masses of young bodies had been summarily thrown onto battle fronts to work out difficulties that European leaders had created for themselves. New war machinery such as the tank and the flamethrower chewed up bodies easily and rapidly, a sickening parody of the factory worker's fate in giving his life gradually to a power loom or a blast furnace. Close to nine hundred thousand British troops died, and Britain might have lost the war if not for American help, at the cost of nearly more than another hundred thousand lives. An alarming number of fatalities were from the preventable and poorly treated diseases that brewed in the trenches. Since the Crimean War, military nursing had developed as a respectable profession, and now phalanxes of mostly genteel women were tending to the sick, the wounded, and the gassed in the hospitals to which they were evacuated; these women's impression of the conduct and costs of the war would have been devastating. At the same time, allied refugees flooded into Britain and required aid at a time of everyday privations and sacrifices. Foreigners were increasingly viewed as bringers of disease, dependency, and dysfunction. In addition to the native poor, they seemed an unbearable burden.

I think it is not a coincidence that *Married Love*, which celebrates the married bond as precious to a degree seldom asserted before, was published during the final year of the war and became a sensation. Hundreds of thousands of women had lost sweethearts, fiancés, and young husbands. It also makes sense that *Radiant Motherhood*, with its soaring, in some ways almost frenetic, insistence that women do exquisite things with their unique biological capacities, became all the rage a couple of years later. Women, new saviors of the nation when so many men had been lost or disabled in battle, needed to make the most of what was left. They needed to take care of themselves and their loved ones because the state demonstrably wouldn't. A rational, if in some ways draconian, plan for producing citizens looked better than the idiocy of throwing them away like refuse in muddy trenches.

But trauma defenses both collective and individual, as natural as they may be in the immediate term, don't adapt well to the circumstances of ordinary life and are apt to poison the future if left unexamined. Depictions of ideal fertile women date back to the Stone Age, but Stopes was the first to use such images in an effort to control the whole process of sex, childbearing, and childcare. Whereas other eugenicists were mere scribblers, Stopes was Wagner. She composed with consuming passion and expected all-consuming devotion to her vision. And she was a canny enough writer, and well enough tuned in to the anxieties of the time, that she had significant success. Take those babies disporting themselves on the grass. In line with the suburban domestic ideal that Scopes did a great deal to shape, we tend to find such scenes charming and natural and harmless. But they are hardly the norm among the world's cultures. The very young child outdoors is intuitively supposed to be attached to its caretaker, high up, as far as possible out of the way of pests and parasites, pathogens and predators and accidents. This is instinctive behavior in a bipedal species, and our quadrupedal best friend supports it. Put your infant or young toddler down outdoors, step away, and ask your dog whether he approves of your dedication to creating a superior specimen. But the image rules nonetheless: Babies belong on the lawn.

This tyranny of images, this demand for conformity to standards that may be arbitrary or even dangerous, has meant that a heavy flood of publicity settled over a hitherto quite private and instinctive realm of activity. The change could hardly be resisted; it was folded in with the real advances in medical care and personal choice that came with the eugenics program, and it seems to have answered collective trauma's need for attention, for reassurance, for, above all, doing things differently than the way they were done when horrible things happened.

The even-more-apocalyptic traumas of World War II were added to the traumas of World War I, and afterward Western society doubled down on the fantasy that women would make everything all right or (*sotto voce* in the purportedly enlightened later twentieth century) woe to women. It does not seem a coincidence that the 1950s era enshrined as its social ideal the same one Stopes had mesmerized her first readers with: the green, conformist, pleasant, high-minded suburb full of women concentrating their energy and brains on being perfect wives and mothers. In America, fundamentally eugenic attitudes went a fair way toward doing in reality what Stopes had done mainly in words, which was to create a self-enclosed world where relationships, the environment, ethics, and institutions served the cause of ever-alert but submissive motherhood and functioned so as to punish deviance.

As a result, hundreds of thousands of women, as disparate as the depressed, unwashed college student Sylvia Plath, repelled by the housewife future being planned for her, and Jacqueline Kennedy as she resisted her assigned role as a smiling, complaisant political wife, paid searing prices in the medical system itself for swerving from the shining ideal: Women's creative and nurturing power must be complete enough to restore everything men had destroyed. Women judged to be failures were drugged, institutionalized, or even subjected to electroshock therapy at high voltage and without anesthetic, which produced convulsions so violent that they could crack the spine. Heather Clark, in her monumental biography of Sylvia Plath, reveals that both Plath and Jackie Kennedy were given this type of electroshock at Valley Head Hospital in Massachusetts, and that JFK took this measure "after a particularly brutal fight about his infidelity."[15] In her autobiographical novel *The Bell Jar*, Plath tells of the "treatment" causing a sensation between a violent drubbing and a lightning strike. Under this assault, "I thought my bones would break and the sap fly out of me like a split plant."[16]

Bored and idle at the back of a junior high classroom in the mid-1970s, I picked up a textbook devoted to advice on physical and social adjustment for teens. It was from the 1950s, but it wasn't far off the girls' Health Education I had experienced through films and pamphlets and lectures. There was a photo of a pretty, slender, neatly coiffed and dressed teenage girl sitting on a lawn and eagerly smiling at something going on in front of her. The caption pointed out her appearance of blooming health and wholesome good spirits and asked whether I didn't want to know her. I remember a sense of deep despair as I compared myself to the girl in half a dozen particulars; she made the grade and I didn't. I must be cheating to have friends; I must be a fool or a criminal to hope for a full and fulfilling future.

I wasn't tuned into the eugenics background, or I would have known that she was on display as breeding stock—not the old-fashioned human kind, that came with money or land or connections, or at least a cow or a goose for the son-in-law, which softened the stock's imperfections in his eyes. This new stock was the entire package, self-made inside and outside, and hell-bent on transcendence, right down to its ability to conjure morning sickness away while pregnant and maintain a body fit to compete with a sixteen-year-old airbrushed supermodel. This stock stood continually up for auction and at the same time was in danger of the glue factory; it was unprotected by a clan or a community that accepted bad luck and tragedy and held that there were good uses for nearly everyone up and down the scale of biological fitness.

Stopes's program—especially her advocacy for contraception—could be lifesaving, health-saving, sanity-saving, and family-saving. It could also be a formula for anxiety, depression, alienation, and breakdown. But perhaps what will prove most damaging in the long term is the political fallout. Here the irony is breathtaking. Stopes's signature contribution to human rights is greater reproductive choice. But when, with her very heavy-handed help, having babies went from something that women were simply expected to do in privacy to something they could strive to do better, spiritually and morally as well as medically, under the supervision of purportedly all-knowing strangers, then fertility was set up to become a political tool. Theocrats, whose views were antithetical to both Stopes's and the enduring consensus of the mainstream, could make just as powerful a use as she had of the premise that the management of reproduction was too important to leave to women and their intimate circles; it required public vetting.

The process now is quite ugly, and the results we look ahead toward could be as cruel and dystopian as when eugenic theory served fascist governments in their rampages. It is thanks to eugenicists like Stopes—because they were the original and long-enduring providers of family planning—that women are on the spot, in public, pleading their intimate personal merits in the cause of reproductive rights.

One star in this spectacle is a pretty, young, blond, healthy-looking, married Texas mother, who speaks of how much she and her husband longed to add another child to their family, and who fears that the medical damage done to her under a harsh new anti-abortion regime in her state has condemned her to infertility.[17] In other words, family formation of just the kind the family-values people themselves are always touting was violated. Her protests are of course unexceptionable; those *are* terrible things the law and its enforcers did to her, and she is entitled to evaluate the tragedy in whatever terms she likes. But her conventionally affecting appeal, her flawless persona as the kind of wife and mother other families are expected to envy, suggests that even the activists who put her in the spotlight have accepted a repugnant decree rooted in eugenics: It's the right of the public, of voters, of taxpayers, of adherents of one ideology or another, to sit in judgment on her, and on all other women by proxy; it isn't simply every woman's right to choose what happens to her own body.

This woman's eugenic superiority is why it's her out there, and not a more typical complainant under the new laws: for example, a single working-class pregnant woman in visibly bad health who can't cope with the children she already has and can't afford to travel out of state for an abortion. Eugenics is in fact why it's *anybody* out there, why pro-choice leaders don't simply insist (as leaders of militant campaigns for the suffrage did), "Women demand their rights, and there will be hell to pay if they don't get them." There is instead an insidious expectation, established by the eugenicists, that the politics of family planning are a spectator sport, a contest between worthy and unworthy women.

As in the past, this is not just a matter of messaging, of propaganda. In an era and a culture in which communications increasingly *are* the battleground, the developments from words are ubiquitous and invasive. They include social workers inside Planned Parenthood clinics, protestors outside them, and fake nurses and therapists in "crisis pregnancy centers," all interrogating women about the circumstances of their pregnancies and their lives, giving unsolicited advice, demanding consultation with family members, and imposing delays to allow for reconsideration, as if pregnancy cripples the decision-making faculty and cancels basic liberties that go with a modern constitutional democracy. Reproductive healthcare providers and advocates certainly don't want all this; some of it they inherited from when family planning was deeply suspect to the establishment, and some they acceded to, step by step, as recent abortion restrictions were enacted. But it's all an integral part of the eugenics legacy.

This legacy has helped put nations with an otherwise better record of women's rights and participation in the paradoxical position of having to wage the war for family planning all over again. In most of the developed world, the technologies allowing choice attract relatively little controversy because they were either invented and introduced locally outside the auspices of any eugenics movement, or imported from abroad when communities at home were ready for them. In either case, they are treated largely as tools for the use of women and families *in privacy*. Family planning is medically regulated in these countries, of course, and subject to social-welfare interventions, but it doesn't get unending outsized attention.[18] In Great Britain and America it is different—especially in America, where abortion is a weighty enough issue to tip the scale of elections. Conditions in these nations[19] strongly suggest that eugenics' poisonous mixture of morality, medicine, and politics is special, a historical distortion caused by a particular kind of collective trauma, and *not* inherent in family-planning provision, and not even in abortion provision. The overwrought drama of Marie Stopes, so destructive in the long term, and all the drama around Margaret Sanger likewise, speak of the way modern Western imperial superpowers understand their destiny in the face of mass violence and mass tragedy. In vast disproportion, they heap responsibility on women.

CHAPTER 7

YOU *CAN* MAKE THIS STUFF UP

Antiabortion Messaging in Wonderland

AMERICA HAS AN ANTIABORTION MOVEMENT unlike any other in the world in scale, organization, intensity, and effectiveness. The movement's propaganda is particularly powerful, tantamount to the Inquisition's in its ability to sic people on phantoms, to conjure out of nowhere grisly threats that latch onto the popular mind and empower rabid leaders.

This is a feat all the more remarkable in a medically accomplished and knowledgeable age, when contradictions to antiabortion messaging sit in plain language in standard textbooks. What (for example) about the need to prevent the "murder" of a fetus growing in a fallopian tube and certain to burst through it, perish, and put the pregnant woman's life in danger if there is no abortion? The fantasy that surgery can transplant the fetus alive to the uterus (where in reality it would cause life-threatening sepsis as its tiny, anchored corpse rotted) is so vigorous among antiabortion activists that it has survived what must have been many encounters with horrified people (like me, a number of years ago). In fact, the fantasy more than survived: It was made into law. In the explosion of antiabortion legislation that followed the overturning of *Roe v. Wade*, the Ohio legislature decreed that ectopic pregnancy must be handled this way whenever possible. It is, however, never possible.[1] You might as well decree the reattachment of decapitated heads whenever feasible. But as often as you say such things to antiabortion true believers, you will see the same half-pitying, half-scornful look, and the topic will forcefully change.

The determination not to engage with opponents must be strategic. The antiabortion leadership would have discovered quite early in the fifty years since *Roe v. Wade* that it is far more advantageous to cultivate a congenial minority audience. Then the 2016 and 2024 elections seemed to vindicate decisively the power of passion, of imagination, of faith-based, sacrificial, one-issue, all-or-nothing dedication in a small number of people. It wasn't a question of how many people agree with *Roe v. Wade*—a solid majority do—but of how many put the issue of abortion at the top of their list.

Critical for recruiting and maintaining true believers has been antiabortion messaging that sought its audience out, that interacted with it, that pulled it in, that made it part of the great drama. In fatal contrast, pro-choice messaging was, until the shake-up of the Dobbs decision, so dull that I struggle to remember any of it from the early period. It certainly wasn't that I lacked interest. I was an activist young girl in a forthrightly pro-choice home and marched on Washington for the Equal Rights Amendment in 1978.

You do have to hand it to the antiabortion movement for energy and creativity in communications. Their messaging is all deeply memorable. It can be found in films like *The Silent Scream*, in mourning rituals for fetuses, in billboards picturing adorable babies, in pamphlets and websites making scary medical and psychiatric claims, and in countless other high-powered come-ons.

As various as these are, they fall into two main types, angry and ingratiating, roughly according to when they were developed. Most of the propaganda that arose in approximately the first two decades after the 1973 *Roe v. Wade* decision legalizing abortion throughout the country sought openly to rouse pity, fear, and outrage; it synched temperamentally with Operation Rescue, a group that organized against abortion clinics in an almost paramilitary style.[2] Prominent were gory films, mass protests with signs declaring that abortion is murder, and self-righteous preaching about the Christian "family values" that were supposed to render abortion unnecessary.

Characteristic antiabortion organizations of the early twenty-first century, in contrast, are the "pregnancy crisis centers" that have spread across the country to offer private outreach to pregnant women who are considering abortion. Counselors (who are often dressed as nurses, trained to operate ultrasound machines, and scripted to exclaim over images of "babies" within "mothers") are supposed to gently and sympathetically evoke "better" feelings, offer material assistance (including shelter in maternity group homes), and beckon toward the "right" decisions: childbirth and surrender of babies for adoption. The public communications of the antiabortion movement in general have changed accordingly. Increasingly, they have stressed personal growth, forgiveness, love, and community. They urge not opposition to what the majority wants—which is legal abortion—but instead support of what everyone is traditionally expected to rally around: mothers, babies, families, charity, solidarity. The movement, moreover, speaks in cozy tones to those who are looking most urgently to belong, to teenagers and young adults. There are lively antiabortion online communities, TV reality series about enormous families, and Lifetime- and Hallmark-type antiabortion movies. The message of these media emphasizes that these are your values, this is your ideal social circle, this is the culture that can nurture you.

But the movement has not grown moderate or gone mainstream in its ambitions; just the opposite. During the decades after *Roe v. Wade*, legal restrictions on abortion became progressively stricter at the federal level and in many states, allowing less and less leeway for those who were poorer, more isolated, and younger, or for victims of violence and coercion. After the *Roe v. Wade* decision was overturned in June 2022, the Catholic principle (taken up enthusiastically by conservative Protestants) of "protecting life from the moment of conception" seemed, more than ever, realizable. A legislative and judicial feeding frenzy quickly confirmed that the antiabortion movement meant business and would if possible attempt to ban common forms of contraception, to restrict freedom of movement and speech where abortion might be concerned, and to extend the legal reach of states where abortion is forbidden into states where it is allowed. There is a lingering threat of a "human life amendment" to the US Constitution, according to which a sperm penetrating an ovum would create a legal person not with rights equal to the woman in whose body this being resides but—if prosecutions and rulings so far in red states are any indication—greater, overriding rights.

The endgame is terrifying to imagine. Margaret Atwood's dystopian *Handmaid's Tale* was published in 1985 and reflects only the authoritarian intrusions on the womb that she could see in news reports while she was doing her research; she had no reason to fear, or to dramatize, the literally microscopic totalitarianism that the tough-minded push to legally protect every fertilized ovum could enable. Minute medical and social surveillance of fertile women would, for a start, be needed to pinpoint pregnancies very early and medically rescue (but how?) the roughly 50 percent of blastocysts that are nonviable, perish on their own, and wash out with a menstrual period that a woman can't distinguish from her other flows. If a deliberate abortion counts as "child murder," then not preventing a natural pregnancy loss might count as negligent homicide, and in fact sometimes does in the antiabortion police state of El Salvador.[3] But that country lacks the advanced medical technology and law-enforcement apparatus that the US could deploy against women to "protect life from the moment of conception." The imagination has to twist and strain to trace the limits of what *could* be done routinely, constitutionally, nationwide under the legal regime that the far right claims is needed to sustain civilization.

It is usual for an authoritarian movement to soften its image even as it hardens its heart and moves to entrench and abuse its power. The Young Turks paved the way for an unhindered genocide of Armenians by flaunting how modern their regime was, how enlightened and open-minded, the last one on earth that would deliberately march a sizable ethnic minority out into the desert to perish. During a time of economic crisis, and in competition with trade unionists, socialists, and communists, the Nazis named themselves the National Socialist German Workers Party and touted a social safety net, even while hunting down their political opponents who sincerely sought reforms. The American antiabortion movement goes so far as to co-opt the enlightened view of twentieth-century genocide and presents itself as the rescuer of millions of the helpless and endangered, the defender of mercy and humanity. Activists are not attackers but defenders; not intruders and disrupters but comforters and guides; not indifferent to demonstrable victims but in some cases victims themselves.

One of the most interesting gambits of reversal that I have come across is accounts of "abortion survival." Prominent examples feature attractive young women who claim to be survivors of late-term clinical abortions, escapees from the holocaust who were providentially chosen to testify to its horrors. They seek to raise awareness of their own past peril and to represent salvation, a role rooted in American Evangelical Christianity but later applied to everything from the drug abuse confession circuit to campaigns to cure rare diseases, with triumphant sufferers stepping forward as spokespeople.

But this mode has special meaning in antiabortion activism. Just by living, "abortion survivors" claim, and by being undeniably human, they testify to their humanity when it was attacked during gestation. It had been a challenge to anthropomorphize a being that, until it has widespread legal protection anyway by virtue of its viability outside the womb, looks more like a tadpole or a stillborn puppy than a baby. For their part, the adorable babies in sign-hung strollers at protests, or in photos on display along highways, or in pamphlets, or on the Web don't evoke more than a shrug among supporters of reproductive choice: These aren't the beings we're talking about. An "abortion survivor" puts a sympathetic, undeniably human face to the movement to "protect unborn life" and can earnestly attest to an autobiography that extends back into the womb.

THE PEER-REVIEWED MEDICAL DATA ABOUT ABORTION survival are relatively straightforward. Extremely rarely, a clinical abortion has failed, meaning that the patient remained pregnant. (In this sense, amateur abortion attempts—such as tight belts, very hot baths, emetics, poisons, and self-wounding—fail all the time.) Sometimes a surgical abortionist has missed one of a pair of twins, and the patient discovered weeks or months later that she was still pregnant; this mistake of course diminished as the use of fetal ultrasound for pregnancy diagnosis became common. Sometimes late-term instillation abortion—done by the injection of saline or another fluid into the uterus, a method no longer favored as it has a significantly worse safety record than surgical abortion[4]—resulted in a live premature birth.

Wherever else in the world abortion is a better-established legal right than in the US and counts more as part of ordinary medical care, the failure of the procedure tends to be regarded as a misfortune or even actionable malpractice. And though the case may reach the news, the public usually doesn't hear from the mother or child in question. In one United Kingdom case written up in a medical journal, an instillation abortion resulted in a child growing up with multiple disabilities. The mother, who already had a toddler, had felt she couldn't cope with another child; she obtained a very late abortion because her diagnosis of pregnancy was delayed by several months. The baby was born alive, but with multiple traumas, and spent seven months in a neonatal unit. The mother claimed him and was raising him at the time of the write-up, but even the careful medical language treats the situation as an extremely unhappy one.[5] In another case, an Australian woman successfully sued for the cost of raising her child, an abortion survivor.[6]

In the US, a story of abortion survival can help a person ascend to a fairy tale of rock stardom, with a stage and recording career and a movie deal. The first claimed abortion survivor who became a media celebrity was Gianna Jessen (the surname is a stage name, and the given name was changed earlier). She was born in 1977 in a California abortion clinic after an attempted instillation abortion. From this point on, the facts cloud up. The Wikipedia page for Gianna Jessen reports that the abortion took place during the thirtieth week of the pregnancy, so perhaps two weeks into the third trimester. *Roe v. Wade* had made elective abortion legal in all states during the first trimester, but most states, including California, continued to forbid or severely restrict it during the third trimester.

According to Gianna's authorized biography, the Christian author Jessica Shaver Renshaw's *Gianna: Aborted, and Lived to Tell About It*,[7] the birth mother, Tina, was a teenage girl who had been discarded first by her birth mother and then by the family who informally adopted her. Tina may have mistaken the stage of her pregnancy, especially since, as the book notes elsewhere, a few years earlier she had weighed more than three hundred pounds;[8] at a minimum, she did not have an ideal relationship with her body. Since advances in fetal ultrasound were not yet routinely applied for determining the stage of a pregnancy, the staff at the abortion clinic she visited may have depended mainly on self-reporting. In any event, Tina reportedly gave birth to a living baby in an abortion clinic, to the horror of the other patients around her, who were undergoing abortions of less-advanced pregnancies. One of many incongruities in Gianna's story is that if she is indeed an abortion victim and survivor, she is a victim and survivor not of a legal abortion but a technically illegal third-trimester one. Any true grounds for complaints about abortion clinics, moreover, will have dissipated with time, as Tina's treatment in a clinic was less safe and expert than is now usual.

Gianna's health presents another foggy story. She was diagnosed early on with cerebral palsy, attributed by the book to damage she suffered from the abortion, but the syndrome is associated with more common severe stresses around premature birth, such as oxygen deprivation, traumatic brain injury, and low birth weight. Prematurity on its own, that is, could explain the cerebral palsy. But in instillation abortion gone wrong, the chemical infusion does its own extensive harm, including to the skin. Gianna exhibits no such issues.

What happened to Gianna after she was born, according to the biography, is even more puzzling. First, however, comes the episode of Gianna's birth, with her mother, Tina, as the cute, trembling, misled victim-waif, who knows in her heart that what she is doing is evil but has understandably been deceived by the proabortion advice she has been given and is now intimidated by cold, indifferent clinic staff. My favorite detail from this alleged abortion dystopia is that the staff do not allow Tina to wear her own fancy new robe but instead direct her to an "unattractive, starchy" hospital gown that is "thin" and leaves her "chilly."[9] Yet once Gianna is born, the staff appropriately call emergency services, write the baby a birth certificate, and prompt the mother to choose a name. As confirmed by the procedures they followed and the documents they created, they were not icy-hearted murderers but healthcare providers following the rules.

In the next section of the book, we meet Gianna as a charming, bright, just-willful-enough twelve-year-old, overcoming by her cheerful, energetic normality the marital tensions in the household. We see her through the eyes of her loving adoptive mother, Diana, as she cooks a delicious Christmas dinner in their idyllic rural home. But at one point Gianna asks, not for the first time, why she has cerebral palsy, and now she speculates that "something more" than birth trauma happened. Diana resolves to tell her and begins to explain what a hard time her teenage mother must have had. Gianna pipes up, "I was aborted, right?"[10]

It stretches the imagination to picture a twelve-year-old, uncoached on what her special story is supposed to be, asking such a question. Reinforcing a skeptical reader's suspicions, her mother now seems to drive a particular message home: "Gianna, I've always told you that God has a special plan for your life. You lived. In most late-term abortions, the baby doesn't survive."[11]

Indeed. This is typical of the book's tone, which renders as outrageous and conspiratorial not only liberalized healthcare for women but the whole of the society that accepts it. There are only two dimensions to the world, the loving and good, and the "pro-abort." To help in this staging, biographical context is selective; important facts are dribbled in with delays and omissions, or overwritten altogether with melodrama. Particularly questionable is the story of Gianna's biological mother, "Tina." Her pitiful but cagey first-person backstory later in the book includes her suffering as a double throwaway and mentions her sexual abuse as a child, the abusive sexual relationship she endured as a homeless teenager, and her abandonment by Gianna's biological father.[12] But the author allows few distractions from the girl's alleged mauling by the sprawling, nightmarish monster that is abortion. According to Renshaw's *Gianna*, the many-fanged abortion industry and its ally the state took advantage of Tina's youth, simplicity, and vulnerability. Unable to present evidence for any of this, the author falls back on distortions and atmospherics, from the alleged oppressive hospital gown the poor girl was made to wear in the abortion clinic to a raft of allegations that Tina is heard making many years later: that the baby's removal from her home was a trap sprung on her, that the conditions for getting the baby back were deliberately "unrealistic and outrageous," that she didn't know she was signing a release for adoption.[13]

In her biography, Renshaw is trying to have it both ways. The antiabortion movement likes the outcome, that the child is fostered and then adopted within its own community after her single mother proves unable to raise her: This is the God-given destiny of Gianna particularly, who carries a special message for the world. But the secular, abortion-tolerating state, which managed and sanctioned this outcome, must not have any credit, and must in fact carry as much of the blame as possible for everything that went wrong, although there are in fact many other causes to point to.

As to the effect the whole episode had on a young woman who was neglected, rejected, and victimized since childhood, the book is just as slanted and coy. We meet Tina again many years later, when she recognizes her daughter on TV, but we hear little about what she has been through or how she is doing. Her fate after losing her daughter was, almost without a doubt, not edifying in the antiabortion movement's terms. Women who give up children for adoption, not women who have abortions, typically have lifelong regret and other psychic sequelae.[14]

But Tina's fate is shown by Renshaw as benignly resolved through an understanding of her past that features abortion as the chief villain—an understanding that allows her to forgive herself for opting for an abortion. Notably, the crucial, heartfelt reconciliation takes place between Tina and Diana, not between Tina and Gianna. Gianna is in fact to be out of bounds for the biological mother who loves and misses her, and who is supposed to be forgiven by her. The two will have no ongoing relationship, purportedly by Gianna's independent decree, which is sweet, brief, and firm. The reader is not let in on any protests, any sorrow of Tina at this decision. Like Gianna herself, she is made to play a narrow, strictly useful role in this antiabortion drama. Even if she were a more ordinary single mother, her function in the eyes of the antiabortion establishment would still be to bear a child for others to raise, in spite of the growing therapeutic recognition that that experience can feel like losing a child to death.

Renshaw's story of Gianna's acquisition and upbringing by passionate antiabortion activists is also patchy and tendentious, and also strongly suggests a human life turned into propaganda. Diana, the devoted housewife and mother, it is eventually revealed, is a "good friend" of the national president of Crusade for Life, who just happens to phone and ask for Gianna's first public testimony, and at that gathering it is announced that Penny, the foster mother of Gianna as a toddler and later her adoptive grandmother, has been the organization's "mother of the year."

A little later in the book, her adoptive mother Diana recalls running errands for a political candidate in 105-degree heat. And at one point, Diana meets a Catholic antiabortion activist who knew Gianna as a one-year-old. This woman, along with Gianna's birth mother, smuggled her into the courtroom during the trial of an abortion doctor accused of smothering a baby who had survived the procedure. Gianna's presence enabled Tina to testify that an "expert witness" to abortion survival was in the courtroom.[15] Clearly, people in the antiabortion movement knew about Gianna quite early, and before Tina lost custody she was collaborating in protest theater that used the child as a stage property.

At any rate, Gianna's fostering, adoption, and early inculcation with antiabortion fervor yielded benefits to the movement that, if they are purely coincidental, would be nothing short of astonishing. The book's go-to explanation is that this is all God's miraculous will, but it looks to me like human contrivance.

How exactly Gianna landed as a foster child with Penny, Diana's mother, is not stated. But how Diana came to adopt her is conveyed by Renshaw (with apparent frequent promptings from Diana during Renshaw's research process: Diana does not hide her eagerness to head off any skepticism and ends up protesting way to much) as not only the heavenly dispensation but also exactly what the child, three at the start of the process, wanted herself. Diana "borrowed Gianna for the day," and the child came back saying, "I have two mommies now—you and Diana." Bonding and mutual adoration grew between the younger woman and the child, but with no bad reflection on the foster mother:

Penny recorded, "Every day she tells me, 'I love Mama Diana. I want her to be my mommy. Then she'll turn to me and say,

'Let me hug you, I love you.' She is making her own break, and nobody has said a word. It is really the hand of God unfolding her rightful place."[16]

In Diana's care, according to the book, Gianna not only grew into opinions and activities uncannily useful for the antiabortion cause but topped them off with compulsive-sounding expressions of joy: The more, and the more outrageously, the cause impinged on her, the more powerfully she grinned, laughed, chirped, flattered, celebrated.

Diana does not hide the ways she and her mother enforced malleability. For example, she gave no quarter to her daughter's information-processing lags (usual in cases of cerebral palsy) until a shocked specialist forced the issue, but even after this she scorned parental support groups. ("[Having nothing to do with them] meant that she and Gianna would have to learn the hard way what Gianna was capable of and what she wasn't").[17] Later, she took her daughter out of junior high for long-term homeschooling. (Gianna had been taught at home for limited periods while she recuperated from surgeries.) One result would have been an absence of regular peer social contacts that could disrupt strict antiabortion beliefs. An end to formal schooling, like other questionable moves, is put down to the girl's own free, insistent choice.

The narration in *Gianna* does not bother to hide that Diana's plan was always to raise an antiabortion pop star. "First, throughout Gianna's childhood, Diana had told her, 'Someday you'll be a great singer, and you'll have a stage name.'"[18] Gianna's career begins in earnest after her mother's impoverishing divorce and the loss of the beautiful rural home. In time she is dispatched on public-appearance and media tours that she often lets the reader know (she makes extensive first-person contributions to what emerges as a collaborative biography) are exhausting and nerve-racking. Teen phenoms without disabilities are often overwhelmed by the psychic and physical demands of the role; Gianna was struggling to stand and walk on her own, to keep up with school subjects that challenged her neurodivergence, and to process losses and separations, surgeries, and other wearing medical treatments that dated from her birth. She explains to one crowd that she is on the stage without shoes because otherwise she will fall. The crowd is friendly, but she is tongue-tied and struggling to finish sentences. She warns another crowd that she might faint.[19]

Yet some of the political fora she stepped into the middle of were highly contentious and decidedly adult in atmosphere, and her mother and other handlers may well have set her up to be confused, scared, and verbally and even physically battered—the worse the better, in producing the most affecting scenes of victimization.

The accounts of these scenes in the book are emotionally tough to read, and the layers of manipulation that they testify to are a challenge to map. I was tempted to make a little investigative project out of my efforts to write more confidently about the background to Gianna's public career.[20] But in a sense, it does not greatly matter whether Gianna's thoughts and words were scripted for her from early childhood, or whether her and her adoptive mother's accounts of events were shaped or reshaped later, or what the precise reality was anywhere in any episode the book represents. What's important is the unavoidable impression of Gianna as a living script.

After she speaks her piece before the Los Angeles County

Board of Supervisors against the testing of RU-486 on local women, she is, according to the biography, taunted and terrorized by leftist bullies. She then becomes a gut-wrenching spectacle as a small, helpless, sobbing, stammering, but brave and persistent object of proabortion sadism.

> Her voice came out determinedly, between gasps. "I am going to speak...exactly...what...is on my mind! I am fourteen years old...and...I am sitting...in front of you...doing...the best that I c-ca-can...to tell you...my story...all right? I'm...sorry. I'm trying...to pull myself together...okay? And I want to tell you the story."[21]

On tour, her young, female, impaired body is used as a prop: "'Why don't you stand up for a second!' [Maury] Povich ordered Gianna, and as she did, 'This is somebody who could not walk, could not crawl.... You're still going through some procedures. You're wearing a cast. Any more surgeries?'"[22] She is clasped and pawed like a talisman by strangers pouring out their feelings about experiences she has been trained to think of as atrocities.

All the while, she strains to present her tougher experiences as the best things that could be. While she is singing among a crowd of youngsters invited onto the stage, a small girl hugs her knees, almost toppling her; she cries out, "I don't want to fall down—I love you!" She goes on a Christian youth retreat and while hiking on a steep hill falls into a nest of hornets. The report in the book: "'It was great,' she says. 'I mean, at least I tried hiking, and I was with people I love.'"[23] The personal costs of her role appear as a Christlike testament to the sublimity of her cause, an ultrawilling sacrifice undertaken to save humankind.

Without the reader being let in on her mother's role in this decision (though the author Renshaw makes no secret of the daughter's fear and reluctance), Gianna becomes antiabortion cannon fodder, blocking family-planning clinic entrances for the very confrontational Operation Rescue, in an all-youngster brigade. At the clinic, she prays and sings to allay her terror, and testifies to a patient escort and a security guard. A screaming, cursing mob descend on her friend Jenny, kick and beat her, and falsely accuse *her* of assault—though she is not retaliating. Gianna feels surrounded by evil like never before and can almost picture the demons. Her mother and another parent watch from a grassy embankment, praying. Eight-year-old Josh gets into a standoff with "pro-aborts" at the clinic's front entrance and is crushed between the door, the outside wall, and a railing, his eye swelling and his cheek bruised. He bravely fights back tears.

The children succeed in keeping patients out of the facility for a few hours, then go on to another facility, where the police take action. Gianna, stalwartly walking instead of going limp during her arrest, is shoved into a police car, and her limp friend is thrown on top of her. At the evening's victory celebration, the children revel in the day's events. The hatred they invoke, Gianna asserts, is a vindication, as the Bible shows.

GIANNA WAS HARDLY THE FIRST "POSTER CHILD," MEANing a real and identifiable child whose image and public appearances are used in a nationwide health-related campaign. These campaigns date from the 1940s, and, classically, children have raised money for medical research on and treatment facilities for their own disabilities. A transition was marked by Karen Killilea, who had cerebral palsy but was raised at home and acquired a fair amount of mobility through physical therapy, a rare achievement at midcentury. Marie Killilea used accounts of her daughter's early life not only to promote better care and better integration into the larger society for those with disabilities—through her books, Marie was probably the most important such promoter of the twentieth century[24]—but also to showcase how devout Catholicism inspired and sustained her family through many years of struggle.

Karen suffered a degree of social pressure and privacy invasion. She was expected to entertain adult visitors who bored and irritated her, and millions of readers had a great range of information about her childhood, from a punishment she got for trying to boss a playmate to the expression on her face at her first communion. Karen reacted, after she came of age, with a dignified withdrawal, giving up her ambitious crutches for a wheelchair and working at a humdrum job at a Catholic institution. But by and large her upbringing seems as normal and pleasant as her parents could make it, with pets, inclusion with neighborhood children at play, visits to the beach, sports, and regular schooling to the extent that it was physically viable.

The eventual evolution of the poster child's role to serve the antiabortion movement looks like a harrowing commentary on that movement's aspirations. Marie Killilea may have burdened her daughter with uncomfortably high standards of behavior, but she raised her to be capable of setting her limits and living a life of her own choosing. Gianna had no such upbringing and no such freedom; she and the political crusade she still champions in her late forties were etherealized together into a single cloud of hype.

The website in her name is headlined, "Gianna Jessen: pro-life advocate. speaker. writer. singer. God's girl. living the impossible." The site contains images and footage of her as a handsome, grinning talking head. Endorsements from George W. Bush and Mother Teresa are prominent. The section marked "Her Story" contains far more inspirational clichés and far less substance than even her biography does—but the impression of forced, anxious enthusiasm is similar:

> Talk to Gianna Jessen for just a few minutes and she's likely to punctuate every sentence with a deep, infectious laugh. Talk to her for a while longer and, as her story unfolds, it becomes apparent that the constant joy has overcome unspeakable challenges.
>
> In many regards, her life has been a short path littered with obstacles at every turn: challenges, betrayal, and cruelty. But for every setback, there have also been invitations into the greatest halls of government. A life that was never meant to be has been used to inspire—even save—others.[25]

A movie "based on" Gianna's life, *October Baby*, was released in 2011 and is an airy blast of pop scented with antiabortion palaver. The protagonist, Hannah, is a glossy undergraduate with cool, diverse friends and adoring, protective, indulgent, well-to-do parents. Her hip surgeries and seizures are in the past, her asthma is no apparent drag, and throughout her quest for the awful secrets of her origins, she oozes sexual tease.

The film's story starts with her collapsing touchingly on stage at her college, where she is the romantic lead in a play. In a glow of helpless distress before a therapist, she slowly, gently bites her thumb. During her hip, wry road-trip of self-discovery with her buddies, she falls out with a totally mean and unfair blond girl and heads off down the road in sunglasses and a rather tight and skimpy outfit, dragging her suitcase with clumsy charm and endearing fretfulness; then her hunky beau Jason pulls up in a rented car to rescue her. The two find themselves in a hotel room together, he gallantly on the floor, she prating brightly about how self-conscious her Christian home-schooled chastity makes her. They wake in the morning curled up together on a couch in the lobby. Their feverishly strained purity has sought safety in a public place.

The magic of Hannah's story as an abortion survivor is bound up with her personal charms and hoists her past every obstacle. After her irresistible pleas, a massive fine for parking on a beach where endangered turtles breed is forgiven; the hotel desk clerk shows a grandfatherly indulgence toward Hannah and Jason when they show up, wet and giddy from a frolic in the ocean, and without enough money for the cheapest room; the sheriff who arrests her and her chaste man-muffin for breaking into a disused hospital in search of her records points Hannah toward her birth mother, apologizes for her arrest, and invites her to visit his town again. His parting advice, "Hate the crime, not the criminal," is a slick adaptation of the antiabortion slogan "Hate the sin, not the sinner."

Though Hannah is plucky, untouchable, and only winsomely sad and angry, the truths toward which she glides are part horror movie, part soap opera, and part sermon. There were, it turns out, twins; the boy's arm was ripped off during the abortion. The attending nurse left her profession because of her trauma, but now, having met Hannah and poured out her shock and grief, she can return to nursing—in a delivery ward now. Hannah's birth mother turns out to be an attractive, successful lawyer with a swell young family; she collapses in a comely heap of sobbing shame and repentance when she finds the scrawled note of forgiveness Hannah has sneaked into her office. All the woman's hopes of putting the crime of abortion behind her are shattered. But of course it is not Hannah's fault! Hannah has forgiven her, as the note states.

Hannah left the note because, during a plaintive visit to the same cathedral in which she was advertised as a baby needing a home (!), she encounters a wise priest who counsels her tenderly about the benefits of forgiveness. After her act of letting go (which might look to someone outside the antiabortion movement more like an act of underhand revenge and the deliberate disruption of a laboriously rebuilt life), she is perfectly reconciled to her perfect adoptive parents, whom she wrongly blamed for their tender withholding of the terrible truth. When we last see Hannah, she is walking off hand-in-hand with the adoring Jason into the dorm where she is now permitted to live, but there will be no hanky-panky, because they are under her father's seigneurial Christian eye, and his will is going to hover over them like God's.

PERHAPS THE MOST STARTLING TURN THE ABORTION-survival movement has taken is that it has become an Internet-driven social contagion. The Abortion Survivors Network, founded in 2012, claims on its website to "empower the abortion survivor community," and urges in giant letters that "YOU ARE

NOT ALONE."[26] Caring help toward self-actualization and a better life are the emphatic message:

> At The Abortion Survivors Network, we provide a variety of resources designed to support survivors on their journey toward healing, restoration, and empowerment. Whether you're looking for tools to help process your experience, ways to share your story with others, or research to better understand the impact of abortion survival, we are here to walk alongside you. Our resources include access to support, survivor stories that offer encouragement, and educational materials to equip you with the knowledge to advocate for yourself and others. You are not alone, and we are committed to providing the support you need to thrive.

Marginal Internet-centered groupings as various as white-power Christians, defenders of anorexia, and purported abortion survivors show similar structure and psychology. Abortion-survival leaders behave in a familiar way in presenting a new, allegedly integral, meaningful, and widespread but in fact rather far-fetched identity in order to exploit loneliness, alienation, suspicion, and fear. A small cadre of attractive and articulate influencers imply a promise that those who join and support them, embracing the momentous identity, will get the same attention and material rewards as themselves through the open channel of the Web. This is supposed to be a "community," not a typical media enterprise in which power and profit are a zero-sum game. The key commodity being mined is trust, and it is refined into the capacity to raise money, turn out crowds, recruit volunteers, apply political pressure, marshal votes.

Though I have seen some eye-popping claims for the total number of claimed abortion survivors in the US, the number who have achieved jobs or multiple public appearances is evidently quite small, and their allergy to public skepticism—which they paint as an attack on their humanity—adds to the impression of a sort of pyramid scheme, one that amasses not mainly the money of the credulous but their cultlike devotion.[27]

The automatonlike political mood of the abortion-survivor movement is ominous, given the proven ability of the antiabortion machine to spring ruinous new ultraconservative constituencies on national decision-making, seemingly out of nowhere. An example is the Old Order Amish, who overcame their religious aversion to voting at the behest of the Republican operatives mobilizing them around the single issue of abortion for the benefit of the MAGA cause in the swing state of Pennsylvania and elsewhere.

In a larger sense, the abortion-survivor movement seems to represent something extreme, dire, and culminating in messaging about fertility. More than two thousand years ago, rhetoric began to foist on women the sole blame for choices about which they had virtually no choice. Worse, women were supposed to be holding the fate of the world in their wombs and abusively undermining the future of civilization and the triumph of good over evil by making the wrong choices. Men with their wars, their tyrannies, their continent-skewing enterprises of greed and corruption were not held to be at all comparable in their destructiveness.

But antichoice messaging was to become even more ambitious as modern ideologies and their communications tools developed. The propaganda of totalitarianism, by definition, takes everything. It moves beyond mere scapegoating or distraction, beyond mere pretext for persecuting rivals for power and influence, beyond mere neurotic fantasy that happens to serve the interests of a regime, beyond mere defiance of important but inconvenient facts. The totalitarian impulse seeks to create a whole thought system, a system of ethics, a social system, a coherent world with an exclusive claim to common sense, logic, decency, compassion, and responsibility.

This is Gianna's world, God's kingdom that the "pro-aborts" assault; it is sealed off and inviolable in her mind and in the minds of everyone close to her. The spreading of the word about abortion survival, the recruiting of victims, comforters, healers, sympathizers, and more spreaders of the word are efforts to solidify a whole false world around the idea of abortion as the great enemy of humankind. Identity, embodiment, and action are added to communications, and the new world rises in susceptible minds as if it were natural, not manufactured, and as if it properly commanded commitment.

In the twenty-first century, we would be fools to picture our freedom, and a life worth living, as depending only on the debates we hear in public, which purport to decide elections and explain court decisions quite straightforwardly. We need to take account of information warfare in its most sophisticated, most insidious, most powerful form ever. We need to know what people are actually made to believe about the female body, and what those beliefs can incite them to do.

ACKNOWLEDGMENTS

I am grateful to the Classics Department of the University of Pennsylvania for their generous appointment of me as a visiting researcher, and to the staff of the Penn libraries and the Yale Beinecke Library for their kind help. I am indebted also to the Guttmacher Institute for their invaluable research into the politics and practicalities of family planning. And Tom, your name is *always* mentioned: I could do nothing without your loving encouragement and support.

NOTES

CHAPTER 1: DAWN OF THE DICKS

1. Hesiod, *Works and Days*, lines 376–77.
2. Riddle, *Contraception and Abortion*, 62–64.
3. Exodus 21:22–23. Here, interestingly, the "harm" designated as critical is physical harm to the woman; that is punishable in kind and in proportion (the "eye for an eye" standard), but the mere destroyer of her fetus incurs only a fine.
4. Ovid, *The Art of Love* 2.719–724.
5. The poems are *Amores* ("Loves") 2.13–14, and I have translated them myself here from Booth's Latin text and with the help of his notes.
6. Isis was a mother-goddess indigenous to Egypt, but at this stage of history she was worshipped in many far-flung places in the Roman Empire, and certainly in Rome. Here she is invoked in proper ritual fashion, with mention of her major cult centers, other gods associated with her, and details of her rites.
7. A Greek goddess of childbirth.
8. The third part of Ovid's three-part Roman name.
9. An exception postdates him: It is the Greek novelist Chariton in his mid-first-century CE novel *Chaereas and Callirhoe* (2.8.6–2.9.6). The heroine Callirrhoe, a captive, pregnant aristocrat, has an anguished dilemma over whether an abortion would be preferable to giving birth in slavery and thus to a slave.
10. Anal sex was the only male method of birth control I am aware of, and since men themselves considered it painful and degrading to the receiving partner, they hesitated to propose it to women above the brothel level.
11. Deucalion is the Noah of Greek mythology. After arriving safely on dry land after the cataclysmic flood, he and his wife obey a divine com-

mand to throw many stones onto the ground; each stone turns into a person, regenerating humankind.

12. Thetis was the mother of Achilles, the most powerful of the Greek warriors besieging Troy.

13. A princess in pre-Roman Italy, Ilia was raped by the god Mars and gave birth to Romulus and Remus; Romulus was the founder of Rome and its first king.

14. Aeneas, a Trojan hero who settled in Italy with his band of fellow refugees after the fall of Troy but some centuries before the city of Rome itself was built, is the legendary first ancestor of the Roman nation. Julius Caesar and his heir the first Roman emperor Augustus traced their family line back to Aeneas and claimed divine ancestry through him as the son of Venus and the mortal prince Anchises.

15. Medea, a barbarian princess with magical powers, killed her two sons by her husband the Greek hero Jason when he resolved to divorce her and marry the daughter of a Greek king.

16. After King Tereus of Thrace kidnapped, raped, and mutilated his young sister-in-law Philomela, his wife Procne avenged her by killing their son Itys and serving him to his father in a stew.

17. Certainly a pregnant courtesan had more to worry about. But even wrinkles were not a vacuous or vain consideration, as Ovid knew. Book 3 of his *Art of Love*, a didactic poem for sex-workers, stresses how extremely competitive the sex trade was, a buyer's market. He advises women, when a flirtation is consummated, to choose a sexual position that will hide flaws and show beauties, the implication being that even in moments of ecstasy they must not forget that they are undergoing quality control. A woman with wrinkles on her belly from childbirth should sit on a man "like a swift Parthian [bowman] turning backwards on his horse" (785–786)—not of course the perfect position for intimacy.

18. Not consistently true, of course.

19. Vergil, *Georgics* 2.532–35.

20. The antiabortion material I have collected includes a thin book that makes such a claim in its title: *Abortion: The Greatest Crime in History*, by Dennis Corle, as "Evangelist, Editor of *Revival Fires!*" Corle's attitude is starting to play out in the American legal system. In certain states, for example, absent appeals-court relief that does not seem imminent, a doctor could face life imprisonment for aborting a nonviable fetus that threatens the mother's life.

21 Ovid, *Tristia* 2.1.207.
22 The Romans were not hampered by the modern kind of biological racism and were quite open to collaboration with foreigners; much of Rome's matchless army was recruited abroad, and some recruits earned citizenship through their service.
23 For example, Lucan, a poet of the Neronian era—that is, four emperors later than Augustus—wrote an epic poem, *The Civil War*, which showed Julius Caesar as superhuman in his ruthlessness and the conflict as monstrous in scale and ferocity.
24 Four hundred years before Ovid's poems, the comedian Aristophanes skewered the absurdity of blaming immured women for men's disastrous handling of public affairs. In the play *Lysistrata*, a pompous government official cites a chant from a women's traditional religious celebration, overheard by accident, as cursing the Athenian legislature's decision to start what turned out to be a remarkably self-destructive military campaign in the course of the Peloponnesian War, Greece's version of a long, foolish civil conflict.

CHAPTER 2. PREGNANT AND FOOT-WASHING AND IN THE KITCHEN

1 Juvenal, *Satires* 6.592–609.
2 Apuleius, *The Golden Ass* 2.2, translated in *The Golden Ass* (Yale University Press), 22–23.
3 The Church Fathers comprise scores of writers, dating from the late first century CE into the medieval period, but the most important ones were active in the third, fourth, and early fifth centuries, when they established key Christian doctrine and practices; see my next chapter, on Augustine of Hippo (354–430).
4 Tertullian, *Apology* 9.8, *On the Soul*, 27.
5 The position enshrined in early canon (or church) law was that an abortion was a punishable killing only after the "quickening," the point at which the pregnant women can first feel fetal movements. This physical transition was associated with "ensoulment": It was a God-given soul that made a fetus human and thus not a creature that humans were permitted to dispose of. It was not until 1869 that the Vatican decreed, in the papal bull *Apostolicae Sedis Moderationi*, the removal

of this distinction, opening the way for harsh punishment of abortion at an early stage.

6 This meant that the church could punish couples—usually concentrating on the woman—who had sex without the church's permission or otherwise violated the church's rules on marriage. Pagan Roman marriage was a quite different legal entity, based on the consent of both parties, who could enforce their individual property rights through lawsuits when the consent of either party and thus the marriage went away. Roman government had a very modest role in regulating marriage, Roman religion virtually none.

7 Stark, in *The Rise of Christianity*, discusses a whole range of causes for Christianity's demographic growth. Speculation about the role of fertility per se—alongside clearer causes like the Christian ban on infanticide—is necessarily tricky, but one consideration seems compelling. The Roman Empire went from having a few thousand Christians at the end of the first century to having around 10 percent (or around six million people) in only about two hundred years, before the sect was even legalized, which allowed open, unrestricted proselytization and conversion. It is hard to imagine that a high birthrate played no role in this explosive early growth.

8 Apuleius, *The Golden Ass* 9.17.

9 This and further translations from the original Greek of the Pastoral Epistles are my own, based on the text as presented in the Nestle-Aland edition of the New Testament.

10 The basis for this strictness was Matthew 5:31–32: Jesus forbids divorce unless the wife has committed adultery.

11 Romans 16:1–2, 1 Corinthians 11:2–16.

12 1 Corinthians 7:14.

13 Galatians 5.

14 Titus 2:4–5.

15 See especially the "woman of valor," the heroic, public-facing housewife and mother of Proverbs 31:10–31.

16 In his *Republic*, Plato—who is in general no feminist—actually insists that women contribute to the ideal state according to their individual abilities: He lays down the law of *inclusion* in the interest of using the talents of a whole population to the best effect.

17 See Deuteronomy 25:4; Leviticus 19:13, Matthew 10:10, Luke 10:7.

CHAPTER 3: IT'S THE BABY, STUPID

1. 1 Corinthians 7:1–7, 7:32–34. This was written in response to those who wondered whether *any* Christians should marry; clearly the preference for celibacy had already had a vigorous start, perhaps stemming from the Essene sect in Judea that appears to have influenced Jesus's teachings.
2. Fox, *Augustine: Conversions to Confessions*, 78. I add to Fox's calculations that Augustine indicates over and over in the *Confessions* that his sex drive was unrelenting: The couple would have been coupling constantly.
3. Augustine, *Confessions* 8.27, translated in *Confessions* (Yale University Press), 233–34.
4. Augustine, *The City of God* 14.10–26.
5. Augustine, *Confessions* 10.41, 316.
6. Those who sought the monastic life could not be married already: The church did not (and still does not) authorize leaving a wife for a celibate vocation.
7. This is my own translation from the Latin text, section 4. I consulted Tarsicius J. van Bavel and Raymond Canning's *The Rule of Saint Augustine: Masculine and Feminine Versions* (Cisterian Publications, 1996).
8. Augustine, *Rule* 6.1–2.
9. Augustine, *Confessions* 3.5.
10. There is a verse about a lustful look being "adultery" already committed "in the heart" (Matthew 5:28), which once upon a time inspired Jimmy Carter to confess in public his excessively conscientious worry about stirrings for women who were not Rosalynn. But the verse's mistranslation and misinterpretation to indicate that there was something unique and dire about sexual covetousness (as opposed to every other kind of covetousness) were established under the influence of this very kind of sexual paranoia in the early Christian period. The Jesus of the Gospels seems to be talking about the kind of predatory gaze that could also be directed at a cow or a field and signal the mood that propels other crimes, such as theft and murder. See Ruden, *The Gospels: A New Translation*, 79–80.

CHAPTER 4: HAMMERED

1. Augustine, *Confessions* 9.19.
2. An arm and a function of the Catholic Church that had been used to prosecute "heresy" (from the Greek word for "choice"), or views and practices forbidden by church authorities, since the twelfth century.
3. Some breakdowns from available records can be found in demographic tables in Levack, *The Witch-Hunt in Early Modern Europe*, 20, 124, 129, 132.
4. Particularly important sects were the Waldensians and the Cathars. The former survived to meld with Calvinists during the Renaissance, but the latter were brutally suppressed in the thirteenth and early fourteenth centuries. Two scholars and martyrs, John Wycliffe (c. 1328–1384) and Jan Hus (c. 1369–1415) prepared the way for the Protestant Reformation in England and in Slavic Central Europe respectively. Papal corruption was notorious, and the papal wars were numerous. The Vatican's internal conflict was crowned by a full schism that lasted from 1378 until 1417, during which time there were two competing papal courts, at Rome and Avignon.
5. The conventional English translation is *The Hammer of Witches*, but this does not convey the sweeping concept of *women* as *evil-doers*, not just wielders of sorcery or magic, which in modern Western thinking can be used for good. The version of the work I will cite throughout this chapter is Mackay, *Hammer of Witches*.
6. Levack, *The Witch-Hunt in Early Modern Europe*, 132.
7. Mackay, *Hammer of Witches* 169–70, sections 44C–44D.
8. Mackay, *Hammer of Witches* 12–13.
9. I wanted to see an early version, and I had a choice among several at Yale's Beinecke Library. Thanks, kindly Beinecke librarians! If I wanted to handle a Gutenberg Bible, I would have to go much farther than ten miles and do far more than sign myself into a database, show ID, and put my backpack in a locker.
10. Mackay *Hammer of Witches* 369–70, sections 138D–139B.
11. Mackay, *Hammer of Witches* 366–75, sections 137B–141D.
12. Shepherd, "Maine Republican Blames . . . Abortion Law."

CHAPTER 5: HELL'S BELLS

1. It looks as if there was a certain family tradition at play. Dickens's maternal grandfather fled the country after being caught embezzling, and pleaded the burdens of *his* eight children.
2. Miles survives by, among other things, feeding parts of his body to starving dogs and changing his wealthy patron's drool buckets.
3. Tomalin, *The Invisible Woman*.
4. Cohen, *Lewis Carroll: A Biography*, 54–55.
5. It is a cogent objection that there is no evidence of a conspiracy here, of any planned and concerted effort to make the lower-class population larger and thus more easily exploitable during this period. But George Orwell in *The Road to Wigan Pier* (90), writing about the early twentieth century British economy, has an intuitively persuasive idea for how the suffering working class is kept down. The governing class as he knows it is not smart enough to connive sweeping arrangements, but an "unconscious process" can be at work. Based on similar observations to Orwell's, I would argue about Victorian fertility that the wishes of the powerful were indirectly expressed in the character of the fiction they praised and promoted, though these wishes were not explicit or terribly effective.
6. Rudyard Kipling, "The Widow at Windsor" in *Norton Anthology of Poetry*, ed. Alexander W. Allison et al., 3rd ed. (W. W. Norton, 1970), 869.
7. "A Christmas Carol," in Dickens, *Christmas Books*, 50.
8. Stengers and Van Neck, *Masturbation: History of a Great Terror*. Particularly interesting is the purchase that the campaign achieved in institutions; it helped shape notorious features of boys' boarding schooling, such as cold showers, lack of privacy, and an inadequate, low-protein diet, as well as dedicated anti-masturbation inquisitions like the one George Orwell describes in his memoir "Such, Such Were the Joys."
9. Dickens, "The Chimes," in *Christmas Books*, 90.
10. Dickens, "The Chimes," 93.
11. Dickens, "The Chimes," 93.
12. Dickens, "The Chimes," 98.
13. Dickens, "The Chimes," 103–104.

14　Dickens, "The Chimes," 138.
15　Dickens, "The Chimes," 128.
16　Dickens, "The Chimes," 128–29.
17　Augustine in the *Confessions* (7.8) did, in a way, say it: A slave born at the same time as the son of a noble house is fated to live under a heavy yoke not because of the stars under which he was born but because of the social position in which he was born.
18　Dickens novels first spread through the United States in Wild-West mode: The copyrights were ignored, and the books were essentially stolen by canny publishing entrepreneurs. Midwestern rural ancestors like mine and urban immigrant ancestors like my husband's would cheaply acquire complete sets of Dickens as a matter of course; they were *the* books to have, after the Bible. My husband and I inherited multiple sets between us.
19　Through the Quakers in Cape Town—one of whom helped found a shelter for abandoned and runaway girls—I learned about homeless children. At one point, the Friends hosted as a speaker a leading local advocate for runaways and throwaways, who told us that a child who could get off the street and into a safe home within two weeks had a decent chance of staying in school and out of trouble and developing lasting relationships; if homeless for longer, a child was "gone." (That was a euphemism, as I found. A panhandling girl of about seven, for example, if asked her name, may reply, "You wanna fuck?") I interviewed the shelter's star alumna, a social worker who recalled the state-of-the-art practices there, including a year of play therapy through which to decompress before trying school. But every other girl who started out in the shelter with her—it had just opened at the time—went back to the street.

CHAPTER 6: THIS LOOKS ODDLY FAMILIAR

1　Darwin, *The Descent of Man*, 207.
2　In America, the Immigration Act or Johnson-Reed Act of 1924 drastically cut immigration from Eastern and Southern Europe. Many thousands of people were forcefully sterilized under the authority of a Supreme Court ruling in *Buck v. Bell* of 1927. In Britain the Mental Deficiency Act of 1913 provided for the incarceration of designated

people, but a later bill to provide for their "voluntary" sterilization failed to pass.
3. I need to disclose that MSI Reproductive Choices is my own favorite charity.
4. The greatest scientific goof of the eugenicists, a worship of genetic "purity," was one that Darwin had avoided, drawing on evidence from plant and animal breeding: Inbreeding in the quest to reproduce and refine more valued traits will, at least eventually, produce sicklier, weaker, more flawed specimens; hybrid vigor tends to result from genetic diversity. Darwin was informed and open-minded enough to suspect that his own children's health was fragile (three died before the age of eleven) because their mother was his first cousin. Marie Stopes was bigoted and ignorant enough to want "half-castes," or the children of whites and people of color, sterilized.
5. See Hall, *Marie Stopes: A Biography*.
6. See, for example, Wood-Allen, *What a Young Girl Ought to Know*. The answer to the title's question seems to be that a young girl ought to know very little and feel nothing but reverence for the phalanx of religious and moral blowhards and battle-axes whose endorsements and scary pictures are arrayed at the front of the book.
7. Stopes, *Radiant Motherhood*, 1–4.
8. Stopes, *Radiant Motherhood*, 78–79.
9. Stopes, *Radiant Motherhood*, 64–66.
10. Stopes, *Radiant Motherhood*, 19.
11. Stopes, *Radiant Motherhood*, 49, 26.
12. Stopes, *Radiant Motherhood*, 141.
13. Stopes, *Radiant Motherhood*, 195–96.
14. Stopes, *Radiant Motherhood*, 203–205.
15. Clark, *Red Comet*, 267–68.
16. Plath, *Bell Jar*, 161.
17. This is Amanda Zurawski, who is not the only personal witness to the effects of harsh new antiabortion laws but is the most prolific one. Her most famous appearance was at the 2024 Democratic National Convention, with her handsome husband standing beside her.
18. This is the case even in Ireland, where there was a draconian law against abortion until 2018. A recent CNN article covered problems in abortion access after the referendum that overturned the law by

an overwhelming majority vote. (Niamh Kennedy and Emily Blumenthal, "Five Years After Ireland's Historic Abortion Referendum, Access to Care Is Still 'Patchy,'" CNN World, May 25, 2023). What is not mentioned is what has barely manifested: any political push to revisit the issue. The antiabortion movement in Ireland has virtually disappeared—or retreated into the shrinking religious and cultural realm in which it was based. It never had the independent political virulence that eugenics gave it in the Anglo-American environment.
19 Including clinic protests so well organized, persistent, and aggressive that they have required targeted law to allow patients into buildings and protect them from assault, harassment, and medical privacy invasion and blackmail when their photos are taken and published. In England, Scotland, and Wales, laws now mandate "protection zones" around clinics prohibiting a number of disruptive activities. In the US, protection includes the federal Freedom of Access to Clinic Entrances Act and a number of laws at the state level.

CHAPTER 7 YOU *CAN* MAKE THIS STUFF UP

1 "New Ohio Bill Falsely Suggests."
2 Founded in 1986 to coordinate mass sit-ins and blockades at family-planning clinics, Operation Rescue was plagued by lawsuits and prosecutions and was blamed for incitement after the bombings of clinics and the murder of abortion providers.
3 Nolan, "Innocents," 55–68.
4 Grimes and Schulz, "Morbidity and Mortality," 505–14.
5 Clark et al., "An Infant Who Survived Abortion," 73–74.
6 "Mother Wins Payout for Failed Abortion." In the developed world beyond America, an exception to regarding a failed abortion mainly as a clinical or legal problem is the so-called Oldenburg Baby, a German Down syndrome child who survived a late abortion and was adopted by a couple who made him the basis of their (unsuccessful) campaign against late-term abortions (Scally, "Man Who Survived Abortion Dies").
7 Renshaw, *Gianna: Aborted*.
8 Renshaw, *Gianna: Aborted*, 177.
9 Renshaw, *Gianna: Aborted*, 3.

10 Renshaw, *Gianna: Aborted*, 14–15.
11 Renshaw, *Gianna: Aborted*, 16.
12 Renshaw, *Gianna: Aborted*, 176–78.
13 Renshaw, *Gianna: Aborted*, 180.
14 The website for the Origins Canada support organization lists some of the voluminous medical and psychiatric literature on the subject, under the heading "Adoption Trauma: The Damage to Relinquishing Mothers."
15 Renshaw, *Gianna: Aborted*, 51, 59, 147–48.
16 Renshaw, *Gianna: Aborted*, 25–26.
17 Renshaw, *Gianna: Aborted*, 40.
18 Renshaw, *Gianna: Aborted*, 45.
19 Renshaw, *Gianna: Aborted*, 91–92, 135–136.
20 In my youth, when my curiosity and indignation were rife, I worked as a stringer for a Cape Town–based magazine called *noseweek*—a serious anticorruption outfit, despite that title.
21 Renshaw, *Gianna: Aborted*, 77.
22 Renshaw, *Gianna: Aborted*, 100.
23 Renshaw, *Gianna: Aborted*, 140, 197.
24 Killilea, *Karen*; *With Love from Karen*; and *Wren*.
25 Gianna Jessen (website), https://giannajessen.com.
26 The Abortion Survivors Network (website), https://abortionsurvivors.org.
27 Prominent among spokespeople for abortion survival are Melissa Ohden, who founded the Abortion Survivors Network; Robin Sertell, who was for some time its education coordinator; and Claire Culwell, who has a large social-media presence. Opportunity appears, as usual, to go to the most mediagenic people and not to the more plausible victims. The scarring and other damage expected from a surgical or instillation abortion are not at all frequently in evidence in abortion-survival media.

SELECTED BIBLIOGRAPHY

Abortion Survivors Network. 2025. www.abortionsurvivors.org.

Aland, Barbara, and Kurt Aland et al., eds. *Novum Testamentum Graece*. 28th ed. German Bible Society, 2012.

Apuleius. *The Golden Ass*. Translated by Sarah Ruden. Yale University Press, 2011.

Ashley, Benedict. *The Dialogue Between Tradition and History: Essays on the Foundations of Catholic Moral Theology*. National Catholic Bioethics Center, 2022.

Atwood, Margaret. *The Handmaid's Tale*. Houghton Mifflin, 1986.

Augustine. *The City of God*. Translated by Marcus Dods. Modern Library, 2000.

Augustine. *Confessions*. Translated by Sarah Ruden. Modern Library, 2017.

Augustine. *The Rule of Saint Augustine*. Translated by Raymond Canning. Cistercian Publications, 1996.

Baird, Robert M., and Stuart E. Rosenbaum. *The Ethics of Abortion: Pro-Life vs. Pro-Choice*. Prometheus Books, 1989.

Brauner, Sigrid. *Fearless Wives and Frightened Shrews: The Construction of the Witch in Early Modern Germany*. Edited by Robert H. Brown. University of Massachusetts Press, 1995.

Caesar. *The Civil War*. Translated by John Carter. Oxford University Press, 1997.

Clack, Beverley. *Misogyny in the Western Philosophical Tradition*. Routledge, 1999.

Clark, Heather. *Red Comet: The Short Life and Blazing Art of Sylvia Plath*. Knopf, 2020.

Clark, P., J. Smith, T. Kelly, and M. J. Robinson, "An Infant Who Survived Abortion and Neonatal Intensive Care," *Journal of Obstetrics and Gynecology* 25, no. 1 (January 2005): 73–74.

Cohen, Morton N. *Lewis Carroll: A Biography*. Vintage Books, 1996.

Cooley, Alison E., ed. *Res Gestae Divi Augusti: Text, Translation, and Commentary*. Cambridge University Press, 2009.

Corle, Dennis. *Abortion: The Greatest Crime in History*. Revival Fires! Publishing, 2008.

Darwin, Charles. *The Descent of Man: The Concise Edition*. Selections and commentary by Carl Zimmer. Plume, 2007.

DeConick, April D. *Holy Misogyny: Why the Sex and Gender Conflicts in the Early Church Still Matter*. Continuum, 2011.

Dickens, Charles. *Christmas Books*. Folio Society, 1988.

Duffin, Jacalyn. *History of Medicine: A Scandalously Short Introduction*. 3rd ed. University of Toronto Press, 2021.

Erwin, Jon, et al. *October Baby*. Directed by Jon and Andrew Erwin. 2011; American Family Studios, 2012.

Faludi, Susan. *Backlash: The Undeclared War Against American Women*. Crown, 1991.

Farrall, Lyndsay Andrew. *Origins and Growth of the English Eugenics Movement 1865–1925*. Garland, 1985.

Feldman, David M. *Birth Control in Jewish Law: Marital Relations, Contraception, and Abortion as Set Forth in the Classic Texts of Jewish Law*. New York University Press, 1968.

Filippini, Nadia Maria. *Pregnancy, Delivery, Childbirth: A Gender and Cultural History from Antiquity to the Test Tube in Europe*. Translated by Clelia Boscolo. Routledge, 2021.

Fox, Robin Lane. *Pagans and Christians*. Knopf, 1987.

Fox, Robin Lane. *Augustine: Conversions to Confessions*. Basic Books, 2015.

Goldsworthy, Adrian. *Pax Romana: War, Peace and Conquest in the Roman World*. Yale University Press, 2016.

Gorney, Cynthia. *Articles of Faith: A Frontline History of the Abortion Wars*. Simon and Schuster, 1998.

Grimes, D. A., and K. F. Schulz, "Morbidity and Mortality from Second-Trimester Abortions," *Journal of Reproductive Medicine 1985* 30, no. 7 (July 1985): 505–14.

Hall, Ruth. *Marie Stopes: A Biography*. Virago, 1978.

Hin, Saskia. *The Demography of Roman Italy: Population Dynamics in an Ancient Conquest Society 201 BCE–14 CE*. Cambridge University Press, 2013.

Hippocrates. *Volume XI: Diseases of Women I and II*. Edited and translated by Paul Potter. Loeb Classical Library 538. Harvard University Press, 2018.

Kapparis, Konstantinos. *Abortion in the Ancient World*. Gerald Duckworth, 2002.

Killilea, Marie. *Karen*. Buccaneer Books, 1952.

Killilea, Marie. *With Love from Karen*. Buccaneer Books, 1963.

Killilea, Marie. *Wren*. Dell, 1981.

Kramer, Heinrich. *The Hammer of Witches: A Complete Translation of the Malleus Maleficarum*. Translated by Christopher S. Mackay. Cambridge University Press, 2014.

Laqueur, Thomas W. *Solitary Sex: A Cultural History of Masturbation*. Zone Books, 2003.

Lefkowitz, Mary R., and Maureen B. Fant. *Women's Life in Greece and Rome: A Source Book in Translation*. 4th ed. Johns Hopkins University Press, 2016.

Levack, Brian P. *The Witch-Hunt in Early-Modern Europe*. Longman, 1987.

"Mother Wins Payout for Failed Abortion," *Australian Broadcasting Corporation*, March 1, 2006.

"New Ohio Bill Falsely Suggests That Reimplantation of Ectopic Pregnancy Is Possible," *Cleveland Clinic Consult QD*, February 11, 2020.

Nicoll, Jeff. *Strange and Gaudy Fruit: Toxic Theology*. Wipf and Stock, 2023.

Nolan, Rachel. "Innocents: Where Pregnant Women Have More to Fear Than Zika," *Harper's Magazine*, October 2016, 55–68.

O'Rourke, Kevin D., and Philip Boyle. *Medical Ethics: Sources of Catholic Teachings*. Georgetown University Press, 1999.

Orwell, George. *The Road to Wigan Pier*. Harcourt Brace Jovanovich, 1958.

Ovid, *The Second Book of Amores*. Edited and translated by Joan Booth. Aris and Phillips, 1991.

Plath, Sylvia. *The Bell Jar*. Harper and Row, 1999.

Reasoner, Mark, ed. *Roman Imperial Texts: A Sourcebook*. Fortress Press, 2013.

Renshaw, Jessica Shaver. *Gianna: Aborted and Lived to Tell About It*. 2nd ed. Tyndale House, 2011.

Riddle, John M. *Contraception and Abortion from the Ancient World to the Renaissance*. Harvard University Press, 1992.

Rose, June. *Marie Stopes and the Sexual Revolution*. Faber and Faber, 1992.

Ruden, Sarah. *The Gospels: A New Translation*. Modern Library, 2021.

Scally, Derek. "German Man Who Survived Abortion Dies Aged 21." *Irish Times*, January 9, 2019.

Shepherd, Michael. "Maine Republican Blames Lewiston Mass Shooting on God's Reaction to Abortion Law." *Bangor Daily News*, April 11, 2024.

Solinger, Rickie, ed. *Abortion Wars: A Half Century of Struggle, 1950–2000*. University of California Press, 1998.

Stark, Rodney. *The Rise of Christianity: How the Obscure, Marginal Jesus Movement Became the Dominant Religious Force in the Western World in a Few Centuries*. HarperSanFrancisco, 1997.

Stengers, Jean, and Anne Van Neck. *Masturbation: The History of a Great Terror*. Translated by Kathryn A. Hoffman. Palgrave, 2001.

Stopes, Marie. *Married Love*. Fifield and Co., 1918.

Stopes, Marie. *Radiant Motherhood: A Book for Those Who Are Creating the Future*. G. P. Putnam's Sons, 1920.

Suetonius. *Volume 1: Lives of the Caesars*. 3rd edition. Edited and translated by J. C. Rolfe. Loeb Classical Library 31. Harvard University Press, 1998.

Teitelbaum, Michael S. *The British Fertility Decline: Demographic Transition in the Crucible of the Industrial Revolution*. Princeton University Press, 1984.

Tomalin, Claire. *Charles Dickens: A Life*. Penguin, 2012.

Tomalin, Claire. *The Invisible Woman: The Story of Nelly Ternan and Charles Dickens*. Knopf, 2012.

Topalian, Elyse. *Margaret Sanger*. Franklin Watts, 1984.

van Driel, Mels. *With the Hand: A Cultural History of Masturbation*. Translated by Paul Vincent. Reaktion Books, 2012.

Whitney, Catherine. *Whose Life? A Balanced, Comprehensive View of Abortion from Its Historical Context to the Current Debate*. William Morrow, 1991.

Wood-Allen, Mary. *What a Young Girl Ought to Know*, 2nd ed. The Vir Publishing Company, 1913.

Woods, Robert. *The Demography of Victorian England and Wales*. Cambridge University Press, 2000.

Wrigley, E. A., and R. S. Schofield. *The Population History of England 1541–1871*. Harvard University Press, 1981.

INDEX

Page numbers after 191 refer to endnotes.

abolition of slavery, 140
abortion
   in antiquity, 6–7, 10–18, 24, 31
   compared to genocide, 20–21, 171–72
   compared to infanticide, 6, 20, 37, 51, 96, 103, 196
   compared to murder, 110–11, 167–71, 176
   "destructive pessaries," 8
   doctors performing, xii, 179, 195
   failed abortions, 173, 202
   instillation abortions, 173–74, 175
   in Ireland, 200–201
   by "uterine fisting," 7–8
Abortion: The Greatest Crime in History (Corle), 194
"abortion survival," xvi, 172–73, 185–90, 203
Abortion Survivors Network, 187–88, 203
Achilles, 17–18, 194
Adam and Eve, 4, 36, 41–43, 74–75
Adeodatus, 67–70, 84
adultery, 8, 25–26, 38, 45, 100, 196, 197
Aeneas, 14, 17–18, 194
Aeneid (Vergil), 17–19, 194
Alfred the Great of England, 82
Alypius, 72, 23
American Birth Control League, 141–42
Amores (Ovid), 10–17, 23–25, 193, 194
Anabaptists, 87
anal sex, 193

Anchises, 17, 194
Anthony of Egypt, 77
antiabortion messaging, ix–xvii
   "abortion survival," xvi, 172–73, 185–90
   in the American antiabortion movement, ix–xvii, 167–90
   and the Dickensian family, xv–xvi, 107–36
   early Christianity and, 33–61, 63–84
   in the eugenics movement, xvi, 137–65
   fertility propaganda, 24, 115
   pro-choice messaging vs., 164, 168–69
   projection in, 80, 144–45
   the politics of family planning, 6, 49, 141–42, 163–65
   the poster children of the antiabortion movement, 173–91
   in the Roman Empire, 3–32
   salvation through childbearing, xiii–xiv, 39, 42–43, 46, 57
   violence at abortion clinics, 164, 169, 202
   witch-hunts and, xiv–xv, 85–105
anti-Semitism and persecution of the Jews, 89–90
Apocrypha (biblical), 81, 100
Apostolicae Sedis Moderationi (papal bull), 196
Apuleius, 35–37, 40
Aquinas, Thomas, 100
Aristophanes, 195

Armenians, genocide of the, 171
Art of Love (Ovid), 23–24, 194
Aristotle, 100
Athens (ancient), 38–39, 195
Atwood, Margaret, xii, 50, 99, 171
Augustine: Conversions to Confessions (Fox), 83–84, 193
Augustine of Hippo, 61, 63–77, 119, 197
  The City of God, 61, 65, 74–76
  Confessions, 65–68, 71–72, 80, 197, 200
  gay encounters of, 75–76
  his mommy issues, 64–66, 69, 70, 86
  his son Adeodatus, 67–70, 84
  influence of, 82–84
  monastic life and authoritarianism, 77–82
  on slavery, 70, 200
  See also celibacy
Augustus, xiv, 18, 21–22, 194
  Golden Age of Latin literature, 9, 21–22
  morality legislation of, 24–32, 50, 96
  Ovid and, 9–10, 23–24
Austen, Jane, 108, 112
Australia, 114–15, 174
authoritarianism, xiii–xiv, 50–52, 95, 171
Avignon papacy, 198

Backlash (Faludi), 34
bathing and bathhouses, 40–41
Bavaria, Germany, 90–92
"be fruitful and multiply" (Genesis 1:28), 74–75
Bell Jar, The (Plath), 161
Bible, 97–98, 198. *See also* New Testament; Old Testament
birth control, 141
  anal sex, 193
  "destructive pessaries," 8
  forced sterilizations, xvi, 139, 143
  "infant exposure," 4, 6
  RU-486, 182
  silphium, 7
  See also abortion

Black Sea, 9, 20, 23
Bleak House (Dickens), 114, 118
bodies, 4
  ignorance about female bodies, xii, 38–40, 49–50, 52, 110–11, 146–47, 153
  as political props, 179, 182
  veils, 37, 45, 54
  at war, 158–59
  See also sex; slavery; celibacy
bourgeoisie, women of the, 92–95
boys' boarding schools, 199
Britain. *See* Great Britain
Buck v. Bell (1927), 200
Bush, George W., 185

caesarean sections, 110
California, 174
Caligula, 31
Calvinism, 198
Canterbury Tales, The (Chaucer), 93
Carter, Jimmy, 197
Carter, Rosalynn, 197
Cathars, 198
Catholic Church
  Church Fathers of later antiquity, 26, 40, 63–66, 74, 81, 100, 151, 195
  the crusades, 86, 88–89, 130
  deaconesses and women martyrs of the early Church, 45
  early canon (or church) law, 86, 88, 91, 195
  heresy, 50, 64, 87–91, 102, 167, 198
  lay communities and the, 88
  monastic life in the, 77–82
  papal bulls, 93, 196
  papal wars, 88, 198
  the power of the papacy, 86–91, 93, 195–96, 198
  sale of indulgences, 90–91
  the source of Catholic guilt, 66–70, 79–81
  women in the early church, 36, 45

celibacy
  in the Bible, 46, 197
  for the Catholic Church, 63–66, 70, 73–74, 77, 83, 86, 91–93, 99, 197
  misogyny and, 65–66, 93–99
  in modern times, 18, 83
  poverty and, 112
  and the Victorian household, 112, 129–30
Central Europe, 87, 91, 198
cerebral palsy, 175–76, 188, 184
cervical caps, 141
Chaereas and Callirhoe (Chariton), 193
Chaucer, Geoffrey, 93
childbirth. *See* pregnancy and childbirth
children
  adoption, 34, 134–35, 145, 170, 174–81, 187, 202, 203
  the inheritance of biological traits, 138–39, 149
  the inheritance of property, 5, 22, 26–30, 76
  "infant exposure," 4, 6
  infanticide, 6, 20, 37, 51, 96, 103, 196
  legitimate vs. illegitimate, 25, 27, 67–69, 81, 131
  as props, 179
  See also families; fertility
"Chimes, The" (Dickens), xv–xvi, 119–29, 130, 135
Christianity, xvi–xv, 33–61, 196
  adultery according to, 25–26, 38, 45, 100, 196, 197
  "family values," 25, 163, 169–70
  hell, 86, 97
  the life of Jesus of Nazareth, 4, 16, 41–42, 45, 55, 61, 73, 196, 197
  the lives of pagan and Christian women, compared, 34–50, 53, 60, 84, 196
  penitential childbearing in, 39, 41–44, 46, 57
  populist authoritarianism in, 50–51, 95
  Protestant Reformation, 86–87, 88–89, 198
  the Virgin Mary, 16–17, 61, 73–74, 116
  See also Catholic Church; heresy
Christmas Carol, A (Dickens), 115, 117, 126, 133
Church Fathers of later antiquity, 26, 40, 63–66, 74, 81, 100, 151, 195
City of God, The (Augustine), 61, 65, 74–76
Civil War, The (epic poem), 195
Clark, Heather, 161
clinic protests, 164, 169, 202
clitoris, 9
CNN, 201–2
Collins, Wilkie, 126
communications, 140, 164, 189–90
  classical rhetoric, 12–13, 21, 48, 54, 66, 77, 189
  demagoguery, 103
  hate speech, 53–54
  influencers, 188
  Internet-driven social contagion, 187–88, 203
  political lunacy and demagoguery, 102–3, 164
  power and control through, 143–44
  printing press, 88, 97–98
  Roman women in public, 34–35
  "sweet-talking," 49, 71–72
  See also antiabortion messaging; politics; propaganda
condoms, 141
Confessions (Augustine), 65–68, 71–72, 80, 197, 200
conformity, 60, 146, 152–53, 160–61
conservatism, x–xi, 3, 13, 18–19, 30, 52, 55–56, 170
Constitution of the United States, 19, 28, 101, 164–65, 170–71
contraception. *See* birth control
Corinna of Tanagra, 12
Corle, Dennis, 194
Crimean War, 159
"crisis pregnancy centers," 164

Crusade for Life, 178
crusades (historical), 86, 88–89, 130
crusades (moral), 18, 184
Culwell, Claire, 203

Dark Ages, 61, 82
Darwin, Charles, 137–38, 143–44, 201
David Copperfield (Dickens), 114, 118–19
"deaconesses," 45
democracy, 164
Democratic Party, 201
demography, 3–4, 27–28, 49, 96, 156, 196
   immigration and, 139, 195, 200
   Malthusianism, 143
   population centers, 61
   unskilled labor and poverty, 112–13, 115, 121, 151, 199
   See also birth control; fertility
"destructive pessaries," 8
Deucalion, 193–94
diaphragms, 141
Dickens, Charles, xv–xvi, 107–36
   Bleak House, 114, 118
   "The Chimes," xv–xvi, 119–29, 130, 135
   A Christmas Carol, 115, 117, 126, 133
   David Copperfield, 114, 118–19
   his own blighted family, 107–9, 113, 114–15, 199
   Little Dorrit, 131
   the magic-waif formula of, 108, 130–36, 175
   Nicholas Nickleby, 108, 118, 130, 131
   popularity in the United States, 200
   reach and influence of, 133–36
   The Old Curiosity Shop, 130–32
divine providence, 17, 20, 120, 130, 132
divorce, 26–27, 44, 91, 144, 180, 194, 196
Dobbs v. Jackson Women's Health Organization (2022), xii, 168–69
Dodgson, Charles (father of Lewis Carroll), 112, 126
Dominican monks, 91
dowries, 5, 27, 57

early canon (or church) law, 86, 88, 91, 195
Economist, The (magazine), 138
ectopic pregnancies, 167–68
Edwardian England, 146
Egypt (ancient), 4, 23, 193
El Salvador, 171
elections, 165, 168, 190, 201
electroshock therapy, 161
elegies, 9
Eliot, George, 126
England. *See* Great Britain
"ensoulment," 195
Equal Rights Amendment, 169
erotic love, 6, 21, 67, 68, 77, 81, 96, 144–45
Essenes of Judea, 197
eugenics, xvi, 137–65
Eve (biblical), 4, 36, 41–43, 74–75
excommunication, 86
exile, 4–2, 8, 9–10, 23–24, 26, 69–70

Faludi, Susan, 34
families
   adoption of children, 34, 134–35, 145, 170, 174–81, 187, 202, 203
   family planning, 6, 49, 141–42, 163–65
   family size, 4–9
   "family values," 25, 163, 169–70
   inbreeding, 201
   the nuclear family, 18, 27, 84
   as patriotic duty, 17, 25
   power's insinuation into the family, 22–32, 170–71
   the "problem" with daughters, 5, 26, 98, 103, 117, 120, 123–24, 128–31, 155, 184
   the pro-family propaganda of the Roman Empire, xiv, 22–32
   Queen Victoria's royal family, 116

female surgical sterilization, 141
feminism, 140, 196
fertility, 4–9
   ancient Roman fertility propaganda, 24–26, 96, 115
   "be fruitful and multiply" (Genesis 1:28), 74–75
   the Great Mother fertility goddess, 72
   the holy fertility of Christian women, 39–40, 49–54, 74, 88, 90, 96–98, 105
   motherhood and social status, 42–43
   See also antiabortion messaging; families
fetuses
   "ensoulment," 195
   fetal ultrasound, 169, 173–75
   nonviable fetuses, 19, 171, 195
   "quickening," 110–11, 195
   threat to a mother's life, 167–68
   the "unborn life" at conception, 19–20, 29, 170–73
   See also abortion; birth control; families; pregnancy and childbirth
fictional women
   Byrrhena in *The Golden Ass*, 35–36, 37
   the Dickensian victim-waif, 108, 130–36, 175
   Greek heroine Callirrhoe, 193
   Ilia (Rhea Silvia), 14, 17, 18, 20, 194
   Nancy in *Oliver Twist*, 119
   Ovid's Corinna, 10–15
   the Wife of Bath, 93
   witches, xiv–xv, 85–105
First World War, 158–61
forced sterilizations, xvi, 139, 143
Fox, Robin Lane, 70–71, 83–84, 197
Freedom of Access to Clinic Entrances Act (US), 202
freedom
   agency denied, 76, 98
   logic and rational choice, 12, 18–20, 53–54, 66, 80–81, 96, 117, 129–30, 135, 159, 190
   reproductive freedom, 16, 30, 34, 44–47, 134, 157, 160, 163–65, 167–69, 173, 180, 189–90
   of speech, 40, 47–48, 170
   See also communications; slavery
"From the rash ruin of her belly's load" (Ovid), 10–11
Fugger banking network, 92

Galileo, 87
Garden of Eden, 4, 36, 41–43, 74–75
gaze, the, 78, 80, 197
genocide, 20–21, 171–72
Germanicus, 31
Germany, 87, 90–92, 139, 143, 172, 202
gestation. *See* fetuses; pregnancy and childbirth
Gianna: Aborted, and Lived to Tell About It (Renshaw), 174–83
Gilded Age, 138
Gingrich, Newt, 59–60
Gnosticism, 50
God
   the chosen ones of, 92, 176–77, 180
   divine providence, 17, 20, 120, 130, 132
   in the Garden of Eden, 4, 36, 41–43, 74–75
   as irrational when it comes to children, 81–82, 134–35
   sacrifice and submission to, 51, 86
   souls and, 195
   the true image of, 63
   See also Catholic Church; Christianity
Golden Age of Latin literature, 9
Golden Ass, The (Apuleius), 35–38, 40
governance of nations, 18, 22, 29–30, 51, 53, 96, 150, 159. *See also* politics
Grant, Madison, 138–39
Great Britain
   access to clinics in, 202
   boys' boarding schools in, 199
   the Dickensian family, xv–xvi, 107–36

Edwardian England, 146
eugenics in, 165, 202
fertility propaganda in, 115
after the First World War, 158
Mental Deficiency Act of 1913, 200
Poor Law Amendment Act of 1834, 113
poverty in Victorian England, 112–13, 115, 121, 151, 199
Royal Navy, 115–16
workhouses, 113
Great Mother (fertility goddess), 72
Greece (ancient), 3–4, 8–9, 12–13, 193–94, 195
Grimms' fairy tales, 132
Griswold v. Connecticut (1965), 142
guilt, 66–70, 79–81
Gutenberg Bible, 97–98, 198

Hammer Against Evil-Doing Women, A (Kramer), xiv–xv, 90–105, 198
Hammer Against Jews, A (*Malleus Iudaeorum*), 90
Handmaid's Tale, The (Atwood), xii, 50, 99, 171
"harm," 21, 101–2, 193
Hebrew Bible, 8, 81. *See also* Old Testament
Hector of Troy, 18
hell (Christian), 86, 97
Henry VIII of England, 91
heresy, 50, 64, 87–91, 102, 167, 198. *See also* witch hunts
Hesiod, 5, 31
Hippocratic Oath, 7–8
Hitler, Adolf, 23, 95, 103
Horace, 23
households. *See* families
"human life amendment" to the US Constitution, 170–71
Hus, Jan, 198
hybrid vigor, 201

Ilia (Rhea Silvia), 14, 17, 18, 20, 194
Iliad (Homer), 17
immigration, 139, 195, 200

Importance of Being Earnest, The (Wilde), 146
inbreeding, 201
indulgences, 90–91. *See also* Protestant Reformation
"infant exposure," 4, 6
infanticide, 6, 20, 37, 51, 96, 103, 196
influencers, 188
inheritance of biological traits, 138–39, 149
inheritance of property, 5, 22, 26–30, 76
Inquisition, xv, 87–91, 102, 167
instillation abortions, 173–74, 175
intertextuality, 11
Ireland, 201–2
Isis (deity), 10, 193
Islam, 90, 103

Jason (Greek hero), 15, 20, 194
Jerome (Church Father), 37
Jessen, Gianna, xvi, 174–87, 190
Jesus of Nazareth, 4, 16, 41–42, 45, 55, 61, 73, 196, 197
Jewish people and communities, 4, 41, 43, 45, 51, 53, 89–90
Joan of Arc, 88
John (apostle), 45
Johnson-Reed Act of 1924 (US), 200
Julius Caesar, 28, 29, 194, 195
Juvenal, 33–34, 53

Kelly, Walt, xvi–xvii
Kennedy, Jacqueline, 161
Kennedy, John F., 161
Killilea, Karen, 184
Killilea, Marie, 184
Kipling, Rudyard, 116
knights (of imperial Rome), 28, 31
Kramer, Heinrich, xiv–xv, 90–105, 198
Ku Klux Klan, 141

Lamarck, Jean-Baptiste, 143
language. *See* communications
latex condoms, 141

legitimate/illegitimate children, 25, 27, 67–69, 81, 131
Lincoln, Abraham, 133
literature
  clichés in, 13, 15–16
  intertextuality in, 11
  misogyny in pagan literature, 33–34, 53
  poetry of the Roman Empire, 3–32
  rescue fantasies in, 72–73, 131–33, 140, 147–49, 160–61
  the victim-waif trope, 108, 130–36, 175
  See also fictional women
Little Dorrit (Dickens), 131
Little Nell, 130–32
Los Angeles County, 181–82
love
  erotic love, 6, 21, 67, 68, 77, 81, 96, 144–45
  through the gaze, 78, 80, 197
  "sweet-talking," 49, 71–72
Lucan, 195
Luke (apostle), 43
Luther, Martin, 91
Lysistrata (Aristophanes), 195

Mackay, Christopher, 96–97, 101
Maine, 104
Malleus Iudaeorum (*A Hammer Against Jews*), 90
Malleus Maleficarum (*A Hammer Against Evil-Doing Women*), xiv–xv, 90–105, 198
Malthus, Thomas, 143
Manichaeanism, 64
Mansfield Park (Austen), 108, 112
Marie Stopes International (now MSI Reproductive Choices), 142, 201
marriage
  adultery, 8, 25–26, 38, 45, 100, 196, 197
  delayed marriage, 111–12, 128
  divorce, 26–27, 44, 91, 144, 180, 194, 196
  dowries, 5, 27, 57
  inbreeding, 201
  procreative marital sex, 74
  prudery/prudence in, 111–12
  widowhood, 27, 50, 55–61, 71, 92
  See also fertility; pregnancy and childbirth; widowhood
Married Love (Stopes), 144, 147, 159
Mars (deity), 17, 194
Mary of Nazareth, 61. *See also* Virgin Mary
masturbation, 118, 146, 199
Matthew (apostle), 43, 196, 197
McCarthyism, 52
Medea, 15, 20, 194
media. *See* antiabortion messaging; communications
Mein Kampf (Hitler), 103
men
  anal sex as birth control method, 193
  of Athens, 38–39, 195
  emotional dependence on women, 67
  legal and financial independence of, 27
  the male medical establishment, xv, 110–11
  the paterfamilias of the Roman Imperial household, 25–27, 44, 72
  the sex drive of, 81, 197
  socializing male youth, 125–26
"menstrual regulation," 8
Mental Deficiency Act of 1913 (UK), 200
Meredith, George, 126
midwifery, 87–88, 90, 95–98, 110, 140
miscarriages, 7–8, 87, 104–5, 108
misogyny, 29–30, 33–35
  celibacy and, 65–66, 93–99
  the convenient scapegoating of women, 15, 29–30, 103–4, 155, 177, 189–90, 195
  cultlike organizations and, 44–46
  in pagan literature, 33–34, 53
monasticism, 77–82

Monty Python and the Holy Grail (film), 85–86
morality
   logic and rational choice, 12, 18–20, 53–54, 66, 80–81, 96, 117, 129–30, 135, 159, 190
   moral crusades, 18, 184
   the natural and the moral, 3, 75, 97–100, 133–34, 160
   notions of "harm," 21, 101–2, 193
Mother Teresa, 185
motherhood
   for Christian women, 42–43, 49–50
   modern "scientific" racism and, 139, 142–43, 148, 150–52, 155, 195
   weaponized, xvi, 94, 144, 148–57, 159
   See also children; families
MSI Reproductive Choices, 142, 201
murder, 110–11, 167–71, 176
Muslims, 90, 103

National Socialist German Workers Party (Nazis), 139, 143, 172
nations, 18, 22, 29–30, 51, 53, 96, 150, 159
nature
   civilization and culture, 20
   the moral and the natural, 3, 75, 97–100, 133–34, 160
   on "natural fitness," 138–39, 151, 160
   natural law, 18–19
   the unnatural, 18, 81, 151, 171
   what we mistake for natural, 52, 160, 190
   See also Social Darwinism
Nazis (National Socialist German Workers Party), 139, 143, 172
New Testament
   1 Corinthians, 46, 54, 197
   Gospel of John, 45
   Gospel of Luke, 43
   Gospel of Matthew, 43, 196, 197
   Jesus of Nazareth, 4, 16, 41–42, 45, 55, 61, 73, 196, 197
   Pastoral Epistles (1 and 2 Timothy and Titus), xiv, 38–61, 63
   Philippians 2:12, 46
   Romans, 73
   Titus, 38
   the Virgin Mary, 16–17, 61, 73–74, 116
Nicholas Nickleby (Dickens), 108, 118, 130, 131
"Nordic" race, 139, 143

October Baby (film), 185–87
Ohden, Melissa, 203
Ohio, 168
Old Curiosity Shop, The (Dickens), 130–32
Old Order Amish, 189
Old Testament, 8, 81
   Adam and Eve, 4, 36, 41–43, 74–75
   Apocrypha, 81, 100–101
   Genesis, 42, 74–75
   Psalms, 39, 81
   widowhood in the, 50, 55–61, 71
Oldenburg Baby, 202
On the Apparel of Women (Tertullian), 37
On the Good of Marriage (Augustine), 66
Operation Rescue, 169, 183, 202
Origen, 63–64
Origins Canada (organization), 203
Orwell, George, 199
Ovid, 9–21
   the "abortion poems" of, 10–18, 24, 31
   Amores, 10–17, 23–25, 193, 194
   Art of Love, 23–24, 194
   in exile, 9–10, 23–24
   on politics, 30, 31

paganism, 16, 34–50, 56, 87, 83, 100, 196
papacy, 86–91, 93, 195–96, 198
Passing of the Great Race, The (Grant), 139

Pastoral Epistles of the New Testament (1 and 2 Timothy and Titus), xiv, 38–61, 63
pastoral sketches, 23
paterfamilias, 25–27, 44, 72
Patricius and Monica (early Christians of North Africa), 61
Paul Among the People (Ruden), 2
Paul of Tarsus, xiv, 38–61, 63
Peleus, 17
Peloponnesian War, 195
Pennsylvania, 189
Philomela, 20, 194
Pickwick Papers, The (Dickens), 108
Pirates of Penzance (Gilbert and Sullivan), 107
Pivot of Civilization, The (Sanger), 147
Planned Parenthood, 141–42, 164
Plath, Sylvia, 161
Plato, 196
Plutarch, 35
political economy, 112–13, 121
politics
   American religious conservatism, x–xi, 3, 13, 18–19, 30, 52, 55–56, 170
   authoritarianism, xiii–xiv, 50–52, 95, 171
   conformity and, 60, 146, 152–53, 160–61
   the convenient scapegoating of women, 15, 29–30, 103–4, 155, 177, 189–90, 195
   exile, 42, 8, 9–10, 23–24, 26, 69–70
   hobby horses, 30–31
   political fallout, 162–63
   the role of language in, 99–100
   totalitarianism, 25, 80, 171, 189–90
   women in public life, 7–9, 34–41, 46–52, 54, 84, 90, 163–64, 195, 196
   women's suffrage, 19, 140, 164, 189
   See also antiabortion messaging; communications
Poor Law Amendment Act of 1834 (UK), 113
populist authoritarianism, 50–52, 95, 171
poster children of the antiabortion movement, 173–91
poverty, 4, 39, 61
   adoption of poor children, 134–35
   public education and, 59–60
   the social safety net, 6, 55–56, 113, 131, 172
   unskilled wage labor in Victorian England, 112–13, 115, 121, 151, 199
   the wealth gap, 6, 34
Povich, Maury, 182
pregnancy
   birth trauma, 174–75
   caesarean sections, 110
   ectopic pregnancies, 167–68
   fetal ultrasound, 169, 173–75
   ignorance about one's own body, xii, 110–11, 146–47, 153
   inbreeding, 201
   the male medical establishment and, xv, 110–11
   midwives, 87–88, 90, 95–98, 110, 140
   miscarriages, 7–8, 87, 104–5, 108
   nonviable fetuses, 19, 171, 195
   penitential childbearing, 41–44
   premature births, 173, 175
   See also children; fertility; motherhood
"pregnancy crisis centers," 169–70
printing press, 88, 97–98
pro-choice messaging, 164, 168–69
Procne, 20, 194
projection, 80, 144–45
propaganda, ix, xiv, xvi, 21, 29, 52, 164, 167–69, 178, 189–90
   eugenics and Nazi propaganda, 139, 143
   fertility propaganda, 24, 115
   pro-family propaganda of the Roman Empire, xiv, 22–25, 29–32
   See also antiabortion messaging; politics
Propertius, 12

prostitution, 6–7, 9, 45, 72, 119, 123, 194
"protection zones," 202
protest theater, 179
Protestant Reformation, 86–87, 88–89, 198
Psalms, 39, 81
puberty, 30
public education, 59–60

Quakers in Cape Town, South Africa, x, 200
"quickening," 110–11, 195
Quintilian, 68
Quiverfull movement, 39

race and racism
    anti-Semitism and persecution of the Jews, 89–90
    motherhood and modern "scientific" racism, 139, 142–43, 148, 150–52, 155, 195
    white supremacy, 19, 138–39, 142–43, 147, 188
Radiant Motherhood (Stopes), xv, 144, 148–57, 159
rape, 17, 20, 194, 103, 105
Reformation, 86–87, 88–89, 198
religion, 47, 50–51, 53–54
    divine providence, 17, 20, 120, 130, 132
    influence on American conservatism, x–xi, 3, 13, 18–19, 30, 52, 55–56, 170
    Islam, 90, 103
    Judaism, 4, 41, 43, 45, 51, 53, 89–90
    paganism, 16, 34–50, 56, 87, 83, 100, 196
    See also Catholic Church; Christianity
Remus, 30, 194
Renaissance, 83, 86–87, 198
Renshaw, Jessica Shaver, 174–83
reproductive freedom, 16, 30, 34, 44–47, 134, 157, 160, 163–65, 167–69, 173, 180, 189–90. *See also* abortion; birth control

Republic (Plato), 196
Republican Party, 189
Rhea Silvia (Ilia), 14, 17, 18, 20, 194
rhetoric (classical), 12–13, 21, 48, 54, 66, 77, 189
rights
    a fetus's "right to life," 19
    freedom of speech, 40, 47–48, 170
    inheritance of property, 5, 22, 26–30, 76
    reproductive freedom, 16, 30, 34, 44–47, 134, 157, 160, 163–65, 167–69, 173, 180, 189–90
    women's suffrage, 19, 140, 164, 189
Rise of Christianity, The (Stark), 196
Road to Wigan Pier (Orwell), 199
Roe v. Wade (1973), 168–70, 174
Roman Empire, xiv, 3–32, 40, 193, 196
    adultery under the, 8, 25–26
    the civil wars of Rome, 18, 21–22, 27–30, 195
    culture of cleanliness in the, 40–41
    elites of imperial Rome, 28, 31
    the "foreigner" in the, 195
    pagan worship in the, 16, 34–50, 56, 87, 83, 100, 196
    the paterfamilias of the family/nation, 25–27, 44, 72
    slavery in the, 4–8, 11, 28, 115, 193
Romanticism, 111
Rome. *See* Catholic Church; Roman Empire
Romulus, 18, 30, 194
"Room of One's Own, A" (Woolf), 140
Royal Navy, 115–16
RU-486, 182
Ruden, Sarah, ix–xvii
    as a Classicist, ix–x, 83, 143
    growing up in an activist household, 169
    noseweek magazine, 203
    Paul Among the People, 2
    in South Africa, x
Rule of Saint Augustine, 77–78

salvation through childbearing, xiii–xiv, 39, 42–43, 46, 57
Sanger, Margaret, 141–42, 147, 165
Satire 6 (Juvenal), 33–34
Saturday Night Live (*SNL*), 107
Scheuberin, Helena, of Innsbruck, 93
Scholasticism, 100
"scientific" racism, 139
Second World War, 28, 52, 160–61
Semonides, 53
Septimius Severus, 8
Sertell, Robin, 203
sex
    covetousness, 197
    male homosexuality, 75–76, 155
    the male sex drive, 81, 197
    masturbation, 118, 146, 199
    prostitution, 6–7, 9, 45, 72, 119, 123, 194
    prudery/prudence, 111–12
    See also celibacy
Silent Scream, The (film), 169
silphium, 7
slavery
    abolition of slavery, 140
    in antiquity, 4–8, 11, 28, 115, 193
    in early Christianity, 33, 41, 43, 46, 51, 54–55, 58, 70, 200
    wage work and new forms of enslavement, 115–16
Social Darwinism, 138–39
social media, 203
social safety net, 6, 55–56, 113, 131, 172
South Africa, x, 200
Spanish Inquisition, xiv–xv, 89–90
Sparta, 25
Spencer, Herbert, 138
Sprenger, Jacob, 91, 93
Stalin, Joseph, 23
Stark, Rodney, 196
Stopes, Marie, xvi, 142–65, 201
    Married Love, 144, 147, 159
    Radiant Motherhood, xvi, 144, 148–57, 159

Wise Parenthood: A Treatise on Birth Control or Contraception, 144
suburbs, 39, 52, 156, 158, 160–61
"Such, Such Were the Joys" (Orwell), 199
Sumner, William Graham, 138
surveillance, 80, 171
"Susanna and the Elders," 100–101
Synesius, bishop of Ptolemais, 65, 83–84
syphilis, 157

Tale of Two Cities, A (Dickens), 133
Teacher, The (Augustine), 68–69
telos (proper purpose), 18
temperance movement, 140
Tereus of Thrace, 15, 20, 194
Ternan, Ellen, 109
Tertullian, 37–38
Thackeray, William Makepeace, 126
Thetis, 14, 17, 20, 194
Thirty Years' War of 1618–1648, 103
"thoughts and prayers," 56–57
Tibullus, 12
Tolstoy, Leo, 129
totalitarianism, 25, 80, 171, 189–90
Training in Oratory (Augustine), 68
trauma (collective and individual), 152, 158–61, 165
trauma (during birth), 174–75
Trojan War, 17–18, 194
Trollope, Anthony, 126
Trump, Donald, 13
Turkey, 171

U.S. Constitution, 19, 28, 101, 164–65, 170–71
U.S. Supreme Court, 142, 168–70, 174, 194–95, 200
    Buck v. Bell (1927), 200
    Dobbs v. Jackson Women's Health Organization (2022), xii, 168–69
    Griswold v. Connecticut (1965), 142
    Roe v. Wade (1973), 168–70, 174

Index

ultrasound, 169, 173–75
United Kingdom. *See* Great Britain
United States
  abortion access after *Dobbs*, xii, 168–69
  the American antiabortion movement, ix–xvii, 167–90, 194–95
  American women after World War II, 52
  conservatism, x–xi, 3, 13, 18–19, 30, 52, 55–56, 170
  Constitution of the United States, 19, 28, 101, 164–65, 170–71
  elections in the, 165, 168, 190, 201
  Equal Rights Amendment, 169
  the nuclear family, 18, 27, 84
  popularity of stranger adoption, 134–35
  pro-choice messaging in the, 164, 168–69
  suburban life in the, 39, 52, 156, 158, 160–61
  violence at abortion clinics, 164, 169, 202
Urban II (pope), 86
"uterine fisting," 7
Uxellodunum, Gaulish city, 29

Valley Head Hospital, Massachusetts, 161
Vatican (papacy), 86–91, 93, 195–96, 198
veils, 37, 45, 54
Venus (deity), 14, 17, 20, 194
Vergil, 17–19, 194
Vestal Virgins, 17
victim-waif trope, 108, 130–36, 175
Victoria of England, 115, 116
Victorian England, 107–36
Vikings, 82
violence, xii–xiii
  at abortion clinics, 164, 169, 202
  genocide, 20–21, 171–72
  infanticide, 6, 20, 37, 51, 96, 103, 196
  murder, 110–11, 167–71, 176
  rape, 17, 20, 194, 103, 105
  witch hunts, xiv–xv, 85–105
  See also warfare
Virgin Mary, 16–17, 61, 73–74, 116
Visigoths, 61
voting rights, 19, 140, 164, 189

Waldensians, 198
warfare, 4
  civil wars of Rome, 18, 21–22, 27–30, 195
  collective and individual trauma, 152, 158–61, 165
  Crimean War, 159
  eugenics and, 158–60
  First World War, 158–61
  for empire, 115
  papal wars, 88, 198
  Peloponnesian War, 195
  Second World War, 28, 52, 160–61
  Thirty Years' War of 1618–1648, 103
  Trojan War, 17–18, 194
  women in military nursing, 159
What a Young Girl Ought to Know (Wood-Allen), 201
"What use that girls relax, exempt from war" (Ovid), 14
white supremacy, 19, 138, 142–43, 147, 188
"Widow at Windsor, The" (Kipling), 116
widowhood, 27, 50, 55–61, 71, 92
Wilde, Oscar, 146, 155
Wise Parenthood: A Treatise on Birth Control or Contraception (Stopes), 144
witch hunts, xiv–xv, 85–105
women
  of Athens, 38–39, 195
  autonomy, 110–11
  of the bourgeoisie, 92–95
  as daughters, 5, 26, 98, 103, 117, 120, 123–24, 128–31, 155, 184
  expectations of full sacrifice, 59–60

women (*continued*)
    feminism, 140, 196
    inheritance of property, 22, 76
    the lives of pagan and Christian women in antiquity, 34–50, 53, 60, 84, 196
    the new saviors of the nation, 116, 131–32, 147–49, 159–60, 190
    the perfect eugenic woman, 142–65, 201
    their practical and material interests, 8, 25, 87, 141
    the "problem" of women talking, 40, 47–49, 58, 100–101, 103
    in public life and politics, 7–9, 34–41, 46–52, 54, 84, 90, 163–64, 195, 196
    the right to vote for, 19, 140, 164, 189
    the social death of independent women, 57
    See also fictional women; marriage
Women and the New Race (Sanger), 147
women's health
    bathing and bathhouses, 40–41
    caesarean sections, 110
    doctors performing abortions, xii, 179, 195
    ectopic pregnancies, 167–68
    electroshock therapy, 161
    ignorance about the female body, xii, 110–11, 146–47, 153
    See also pregnancy and childbirth
women's work
    American women during World War II, 52
    as midwives, 87–88, 90, 95–98, 110, 140
    in modern nursing, 140, 159
    sex work, 6–7, 9, 45, 72, 119, 123, 194
    wet nurses and nannies, 33, 35, 43, 43, 104, 140
Wood-Allen, Mary, 201
Woolf, Virginia, 140
workhouses, 113
Works and Days (Hesiod), 5, 31
World War I, 158–61
World War II, 28, 52, 160–61
Wycliffe, John, 198

Young Turks, 171

Zurawski, Amanda, 201